MW01153426

Financial Markets

Stocks, bonds, money markets; IPOS, auctions, trading (buying and selling), short selling, transaction costs, currencies; futures, options

Vol. 1

Thomas H. McInish, PhD

James Upson, PhD

ISBN: ISBN-13: 978-1492887171

First edition published in December 2013

Second edition published in October 2014

Printed in the United States of America

DEDICATION

McInish: To Margaret McInish,

and Sheun and Ashley Aluko, with all my love

Upson: To my wife and children, with all my love.

TABLE OF CONTENTS

PREFACE

This book is written for market professionals and students who seek knowledge concerning financial markets. We focus on all four types of financial products: equities (stocks and warrants), debt instruments (bond and money market instruments), foreign exchange, and derivatives. We believe that in today's financial environment everyone must have a basic understanding of each of these markets. More and more individual investors are managing their own retirement portfolios. Both individuals and institutions are investing across borders so that it is not wise to only consider foreign exchange in international finance books and courses.

Volume 1 comprises five chapters. Chapter 1 describes the ways that equities and debt are created, including initial public offerings, private placements, and auctions.

All financial assets have certain characteristics in common. All four product types are traded in markets, and, fortunately, the ways in which they are traded are limited. Chapter 2 describes the various trading venues such as exchanges and alternative trading systems and how trading is conducted such as in batch or call sessions and in continuous markets.

Chapter 3 explains the various types of transactions costs associated with trading financial assets. We cover both explicit transactions costs such as commissions and implicit transactions costs such as the cost resulting from needing to execute an order quickly. Chapter 4 discusses a topic that is frequently overlooked—clearing and settlement. Clearing and settlement involve the exchange of the financial assets and funds that result from trading. Historically, this topic has not been considered important for domestic investors. But as investors invest globally they encounter a wider variety of clearing and settlement practices. Also, the risks involved in clearing and settlement are greater in some markets than in others. Hence, the authors believe that understanding of this topic is essential for today's finance professionals and individual investors.

Chapter 5 deals with the regulation of financial markets. The particular institutions that regulate each market vary from country to country. But countries are increasingly coordinating their regulation of financial markets.

During the crisis of 2008 governments worldwide cooperated in instituting bans of short selling. And efforts to combat money laundering and other financial crimes now have a worldwide scope.

Volume 2 focuses on understanding equities, debt, and foreign exchange. Chapter 1 describes the features of equities. Chapter 2 describes both the characteristics of debt instruments and the analysis of debt instruments, including the term structure, yield-to-maturity, total realized compound yield and duration. Chapter 3 describes foreign exchange markets. Foreign exchange has traditionally been neglected in studies of financial markets. Financial institutions have led the trend toward international investing. But recently the discount broker Charles Schwab introduced accounts that allow individual U.S. investors in trade securities in a dozen countries outside the U.S. in local currencies

Volume 3 focuses on understanding options and futures. These are the major derivatives used by both speculators and hedgers. All business professionals need to understand derivatives. This is not just a topic for speculators or sophisticated professionals. As the population in developed countries around the world ages, they need to understand how to use derivatives to protect their portfolios and generate income.

Hedging is an important concept that all financial professionals and individual investors need to understand. We devote a chapter to this topic and put this chapter in Volume 3 because derivatives are the primary tools used in hedging.

Providing background for writing this book, the authors have traveled extensively, visiting exchanges, universities, brokerage firms, banks, and other businesses in many countries, including Argentina, Australia, Canada, Chile, China, Denmark, England, Finland, France, Germany, Greece, Hong Kong, Italy, Indonesia, Japan, Malaysia, Mexico, Lithuania, Luxembourg, the Netherlands, New Zealand, Norway, the Philippines, Poland, Portugal, Russia, Singapore, Spain, Sweden, Switzerland, Taiwan, Thailand, Turkey, Viet Nam and the USA.

CHAPTER ONE

CREATION OF EQUITIES AND DEBT SECURITIES

Key Terms

Aftermarket—the initial period of secondary market trading of new securities following their initial sale.

Best efforts—an offering of new securities in which an investment banker acts as a selling agent and only buys the securities that are presold.

Bond—a debt instrument typically with an initial maturity of more than one year that is issued for the purpose of borrowing money.

Bookbuild underwriting—a type of firm underwriting in which the underwriter solicits indications of interest prior to the offering.

Common stock—documents that represents ownership of a firm.

Direct public offering—an offering of new equity directly to the public without the aid of an investment banker.

Downtick—a trade price lower than the last trade price.

Dutch auction—a type of auction for new securities in which (1) bidders indicate the price and quantity they are willing to buy at that price, (2) the winners are the set of bidders collectively seeking the quantity offered at the highest weighted average price, and (3) the winning price is the lowest price offered by a member of the set of winners.

Equities—securities representing capital contributed to the firm for which there is no obligation to repay.

Fail-to-deliver—the failure to deliver stock on settlement day, especially by a short seller.

Financial covenant—a clause in an agreement between an issuer and investors that establishes requirements concerning financial variables.

Firm underwriting—an offering of new securities in which an investment banker buys the securities from the issuer and resells them to the public.

Fixed income securities—debt instruments sold by companies and governments.

Fixed price underwriting—a way of selling new securities in which an investment banker sets a price and then solicits subscriptions from investors.

Flipping—sale of stock acquired from an underwriter in a new securities offering during the first few days following the offering.

Float—the part of a company's outstanding stock available for trading rather than being owned by controlling shareholders and others unlikely to trade.

Going public—an initial sale of common stock to the public, also called and initial public offering or IPO.

Greenshoe option— a clause in an agreement between an issuer and investors that gives an investment banker the right to buy additional shares from a firm typically for a period of 30 days after the offering day.

Incurrence covenant—a clause in an agreement between an issuer and investors that identifies conditions that must be met when some event occurs such as an acquisition or a new debt issue.

Initial public offering—an initial sale of debt of common stock to the public; for the sale of common stock also called going public or an IPO.

Investment bank—a firm that specializes in selling common stock and bonds to the public.

IPO—see initial public offering. .

Lead underwriter—the firm that originates the deal for a new issue, has primary responsibility for the offering and is in direct contact with the issuer (see also syndicate manager).

Leaving money on the table—funds foregone by a firm that has an IPO that is substantially underpriced so that there is a large first day price increase.

Locate rule—a rule of the U.S. Financial Institution Regulatory Authority requiring short sellers to locate stock to borrow prior to executing a short sale in a stock listed on the Threshold Security List.

Lockup—a contractual provision between large investors and the underwriter prohibiting the sale of stock in the aftermarket, typically for 180 days.

Maintenance covenant—a clause in an agreement between an issuer and investors that establishes financial requirements that must be met at regular intervals such as quarterly.

Mutual fund—an investment company in the business of investing in financial assets. Investments can be initiated by buying shares directly from the mutual fund and liquidated by selling the shares back to the mutual fund.

Merchant bank—an investment bank that invests its own money in addition to raising capital from the public.

Naked short—a short sale made without any intention of borrowing stock to deliver.

Negative covenant—a clause in an agreement between an issuer and an investor that restricts the actions of the issuer such as prohibiting the payment of dividends.

Negative rebate—the lender of securities keeps all of the earnings from investing the collateral posted by the borrower and also receives an additional payment.

Net interest cost—a method of calculating an offering rate for new U.S. municipal bond issues.

Offre à Prix Minimal—an auction method of issuing new shares used in France in which a minimum and maximum price are set and investors submit bids between these two prices.

Penalty bid—an offer by an underwriter to buy back shares sold in an initial public offering and requiring the forfeiture of the syndicate selling commission by the broker who originally sold the shares.

Positive covenant— a clause in an agreement between an issuer and investors that requires certain actions such as providing periodic reports.

Primary market—a set of institutional arrangements for transferring money from financial investors to businesses and governments.

Private placement—a method of fundraising in which securities are sold to a small number of investors, often a wealthy individual or a financial institution, either directly by the issuer or through an investment banker.

Prospectus—a part of the registration statement given to investors briefly describing the terms of an offering and details about the firm's finances.

Quantity discovery—the process of determining the demand for a new securities issue.

Quiet period—a period of time following an initial public offering during which comments from underwriters and the issuer are prohibited.

Rebate rate—the portion of the earnings from collateral posted with a stock lender that is returned to the short seller.

Registration statement—a document filed with the U.S. Securities and Exchange Commission describing the terms of an offering and details about the firm's finances.

Rights offering—an offering made directly to a firm's current shareholders giving them the right to purchase new securities at a discounted price.

Road show—an organized series of presentations in various cities in which a firm's officers and investment bankers meet potential investors.

Selling group—investment banking firms helping to sell an IPO, but having less responsibility that members of the syndicate.

Short sale against the box—the short sale of a security that the seller owns, but that is not available for immediate delivery.

Short selling—the sale of an asset not owned, typically in hopes of profiting from a price decline.

Special—a stock that is difficult to borrow.

Specialness—the difference between the typical rebate rate and the rebate rate on a given loan.

Standby commitment—an agreement under which an investment banker will purchase any shares not purchased by current shareholders and resell these shares to investors.

Stabilization bid—an offer by an investment banker to buy shares of a new issue to prevent its price from declining below the offering price.

Syndicate co-managers—the term for each firm when more than one firm acts as a manager for an offering.

Syndicate manager—the firm that originates the deal for a new issue and is in direct contact with the issuer (see also lead underwriter).

Syndicate—a group of investment bankers handling a securities offering.

Threshold Security List—a list of securities maintained by the U.S. Financial Industry Regulatory Authority that identifies stocks with at least 10,000 shares representing more than 0.5 percent of outstanding shares with fail to deliver status for five consecutive settlement days.

Underwriting—a type of public offering in which an investment banker arranges the sale of new securities to investors.

Underwriting spread—the difference between the price an underwriter pays to the issuer and the price paid by investors.

Uptick—a trade price higher than the last trade price.

Yankee auction—a type of Dutch auction in which the bidders pay the price actually bid rather than the lowest successful bid price.

Zero-plus tick—a price that is the same as the last price, but higher than the last different price.

IN THIS CHAPTER, we discuss how to raise new capital. Specifically, we discuss:

- Private placements, and
- Public offerings, which for equities are called initial public offerings or IPOs. There are many ways to make a public offering, including:
  - Best efforts,
  - Firm underwritings (fixed price, bookbuild),
  - Direct public offerings,
  - Rights offerings, and
  - Auctions.

We also discuss

- Aftermarket trading of new securities, and
- Short selling.

1. Introduction

The creation of new securities takes place in the **primary market**, the market for the initial sale of securities. We describe how these securities are created in this chapter. A hallmark of the primary market is that the proceeds from the sale of securities to investors go to the issuers of the securities. Thus, the primary market provides businesses with funds to operate and expand and provides governments funds to carry on their activities.

2. Private placements

In a **private placement** securities are sold to a small number of investors. In the U.S. these offerings are generally exempt from registration with the Securities and Exchange Commission. Because private placements in the U.S. are not registered, advertising, cold calling and other solicitations targeted at the public are not permitted. Purchasers are limited to accredited investors, either institutions or individuals, and the size of the offering, or the number of investors (or both) are limited. These private placements are sometime called private investment in public equity (PIPE).

Besides avoiding the need to register the securities, private placements have other advantages. The number of investors involved is generally small. Agreement can often be reached quickly. In

January 2012 the United States Antimony Corporation sold about 1.1 million shares to a small group of investors along with warrants to purchase another 1.1 million shares raised and about 2.2 million USD.[1] A second private placement of 475,000 shares and warrants in June 2012 raised about 2.8 million USD.

A small group of lenders, especially since they are typically large financial institutions, may require more monitoring than would be possible with a public offering. The financial institutions talk to the issuer about its operations on a regular basis and are able to influence the issuer's actions. Also, the terms of the offering can be tailored to the needs of a particular client. And the firm may be willing to disclose more details concerning its operations and finances to a small lending group. Specific covenants can be included in the agreement or a non-standard maturity date can be negotiated. **Negative covenants** restrict the actions of the issuer. They may prohibit the payment of dividends or require the issuer to maintain a target current ratio. **Positive covenants** require certain standards or actions such as providing periodic reports. **Financial covenants** establish requirements concerning financial variables. **Maintenance covenants** establish financial requirements that must be met at regular intervals such as quarterly and **incurrence covenants** establish requirements that must be met when some event occurs such as an acquisition or a new debt issue.[2]

Private placements can be large, but are generally smaller than the largest public offerings. Most private placements have higher interest rates (because of their illiquidity), lower legal costs (because they are not registered, at least in the U.S.) and lower selling costs (because of the larger size and smaller number of investors involved). In general, for small issues private placements are cheaper. However, public offerings may be cheaper for very large offerings.

---

[1] http://www.reuters.com/finance/stocks/UAMY.K/key-developments/article/2466250

[2] Carey, Prowse, Rea and Udell (1993) provide an extensive discussion of the private placement market.

3. Public offerings

Public offerings are used by businesses and governments to sell both equities and fixed-income securities, including bonds. **Equities** or **common stock** represent ownership in the firm and there is no obligation for the firm to repay. **Bonds** are debt instruments with an initial maturity of more than one year issued for the purpose of borrowing money.

Unlike private placements, the terms of a public offering are not tailored to the needs of a particular group of investors. Also, there are typically a large number of investors, which facilitates creating a secondary market. Secondary markets allow investors to sell bonds prior to the maturity or shares of stock prior to the liquidation of the firm. In the U.S. issuers rarely sell the offering directly to the public. In most cases the issuer hires an **investment banker**, a firm that specializes in selling stocks and bonds to the public. In some countries commercial banks are also investment banks. An investment bank that invests its own money in addition to raising capital from the public is called a **merchant bank**. When a firm sells its equity to the public for the first time the process is called **going public** and the offering is called an **initial public offering (IPO).** The terms of the offering generally are the same for all investors and typically the offering is sold to many investors rather than a small group. The process of selling new securities to investors using an investment banker is called an **underwriting**.

Companies go public for various reasons. A public offering can be used to raise cash that can be used to pay off debt, or expand the business. Also, as we explain in detail in chapter 2, liquidity, or the ease with which a security can be bought and sold, creates value. Securities that are more liquid can be worth more. This liquidity allows early investors to cash out and diversify their holdings. A publicly traded stock may help companies to link managerial compensation to firm financial performance. The fact that a company is public may increase its credibility and statue.

Public offerings usually must meet stringent regulatory requirements. We will describe the U.S. procedures. The issuer must prepare a **registration statement** describing the terms of the offering and providing details about the firm's finances. The registration statement must be filed with the Securities and Exchange Commission for review. After a period of time the issuer can ask for the registration statement to be finalized and the offering can proceed. Firms usually prepare a shorter document called a **prospectus** to give to investors. The prospectus, which is part of the registration statement, describes the offering and the finances of the firm, but in less detail.

The offering price is typically negotiated between the investment banker and the issuer. For reasons that scholars and practitioners have not been able to fully explain, IPOs are usually underpriced so that the price increases from the offering price in the short run. A number of explanations have been offered for this underpricing. Naturally, a cheaper price makes the issue easier to sell. But it is not clear why issuers agree to a cheaper price, which is called **leaving money on the table,** especially if the price increases significantly on the offering day. Underpricing may make it easier to sell follow-on offerings, may protect the firm from lawsuits, and may compensate buyers for helping to determine the best offering price. Governments selling public sector enterprises in public offerings may want to insure that buyers earn good returns to enhance capital markets and promote political support.[1]

3.1. Best efforts

In a **best efforts** offering, an investment banker acts as an agent to sell an issuer's stock or bonds, but the investment banker only commits to buying securities for which a buyer has been lined up in advance. Typically, a minimum amount must be raised or the offering is cancelled. This ensures that the issuer has sufficient funds to undertake its project. There is also a maximum amount that can be raised. The minimum and maximum offering size, the price of the issue, the fees being paid, and information about the issuer will be included in the offering document. Best efforts underwriting are suitable for relatively small offerings and for firms that do not have established records. Best efforts offerings are relatively common in the

---

[1] Arugaslan, Cook, and Kieschnick, (2005) examine and reject the idea that underpricing is an effort to spread ownership more widely to reduce the monitoring power of new owners.

U.S.[1] The investment banker offers the issue continuously until the issue is successful or terminated. Sherman (1992) argues that for certain types of projects investors may have superior insight into the prospects for success so that success or failure of a best efforts offering provides valuable business information to the issuer.

3.2. Firm underwritings

In a **firm underwriting**, the investment banker monitors market conditions and the demand for the issue. When the time is judged to be right, the investment banker buys the entire issue and is responsible for reselling it to the public. Hence, a firm underwriting has more risk for the investment banker and less risk for the issuer than a best efforts offering. The underwriters buy the issue at one price and resell it a higher price and the difference between these two prices is the **underwriting spread**. In most countries, the underwriter is required to sell the issue only at the price stated in the offering documents. However, some countries such as Singapore, Portugal, and Japan have allowed price discrimination in some cases. The price offered to employees or to domestic investors might be lower than the price offered to other investors.

The underwriting spread is shared between the various members of the **syndicate** or **selling group.** A **syndicate**, which is a group of investment bankers, underwrites most large offerings. The **lead underwriter** (also called the **syndicate manager)** is responsible for the deal and works with the issuer. For very large underwritings there may be several lead underwriters who serve as **co-managers**. Also, firms may be asked to join a **selling group** to help market the issue. The lead underwriter is typically responsible for deciding how to allocate the offering among syndicate and

---

[1] In a rights offering and a best efforts stock offering, Hanmi announced that it had raised more than the minimum offering amount of 105 million USD and that it would continue to accept subscriptions for several days unless the amount reached the maximum of 120 million USD.
http://www.istockanalyst.com/article/viewiStockNews/articleid/4331469
http://finance.yahoo.com/news/Hanmi-Announces-Closing-Date-pz-1745297924.html?x=0&.v=1

selling group members. In Australia the lead underwriter is the only member of the syndicate with knowledge of all the purchasers of the issue. For some offerings the underwriter may prefer to distribute the issue widely by limiting each investor's purchase. This facilitates the development of a secondary market. On the other hand, if the offering is especially attractive, the underwriter may use share allocations to reward firms that have provided business to the investment banker in the past or are expected to provide business in the future. Allocations may also be used to reward investors who provide valuable information such as help is setting the offering price.

Hoover's, Inc. provides in-depth information about IPO filings, recent offering performance, the upcoming IPO calendar, and other information at http://www.ipocentral.com/.

3.2.1. Fixed price

Historically, **fixed price underwritings** have been favored in the U.K., Singapore, Australia, India, and other present and former members of the British Commonwealth. Until recently the fixed price method was the only method used in Japan. In this type of offering the offering price is set early, perhaps six weeks before the offering date, and the underwriter begins soliciting purchasers for the issue. Investors are required to fill out a subscription document and in many cases must pay for the securities in advance. In some markets it is common for the issue to be substantially over subscribed. Investors may request more shares than they actually want, believing that their order will only be partially filled. Because the price is set early, the offering price must be set to ensure that investors will believe that the issue is attractively priced even if share prices overall or in the firm's industry decline. Fixed price underwritings are typically used only for best efforts offerings in the U.S.

3.2.2. Bookbuild

Bookbuild underwritings are the norm for large issues in the U.S. In this method the investment banker prepares preliminary offering documents and specifies a price range rather than a single price. This price range can be easily changed if market conditions change. Over time the underwriters talk to institutions and large investors who are potential buyers to gauge demand at various prices. The quantity offered can also easily be changed if feedback from potential buyers indicates higher or lower demand than expected. Also, the underwriter organizes a **road show** in cities where the underwriter expects demand for the issue. At the road show potential investors meet company officers and the underwriters. In a bookbuild IPO when the underwriter completes its assessment and judges that there is sufficient demand for the issue, the underwriter sets a final price, files the final documents, purchases the offering from the issuer, and resells the offering to investors as quickly as possible.

3.2.3. Comparing fixed price and bookbuild

It may be useful to recap and compare differences in the fixed price and bookbuild methods. The final price is set much earlier in the fixed price offering than in the bookbuild offering. Hence, there is less time for market movements to adversely affect the price in the bookbuild method. Also, more intelligence is collected in the book build method. According to Handley (1993), in the U.S. the highest and lowest indicated offering price spans a 16% range around its midpoint, providing evidence that there is uncertainty about the equilibrium price. The bookbuild method may require less underpricing because it provides a way of reducing uncertainty. A second benefit of the bookbuild method is that it provides an opportunity for **quantity discovery**, information about the number of shares demanded at various prices, before the final offering price and size are set. On the other hand the fixed price method requires investors to actually commit to buy shares prior to the offering date. And whether and by how much an issue is oversubscribed also provides information. Whether the fixed price or bookbuild method is optimal depends on the characteristics of the issuing firm.[1]

In the book build method the underwriter has discretion about who purchases the shares. In the fixed price method share allocations can be non-discretionary as in Finland, France, Hong Kong and Singapore or discretionary as in Australia, Brazil, Germany and best efforts in the U.S.

---

[1] Benveniste and Busaba (1997).

3.3. Direct public offering

During the dot-com bubble at the end of the 1990s there was an interest in **direct public offerings** (DPO) in which a company sells its shares directly to investors without an underwriter. Spring Street Brewing was one on the first companies to go public by using a DPO, raising about 2 million USD in 1996.[1] Internet Ventures, Inc., a provider of internet services, raised 5 million USD in a direct IPO in 1997.[2] However these early efforts had limited success, and, according to Sjostrom (2001), less than 40% of internet DPOs result in the companies raising any money and the author concludes that a small company should view an internet DPO as only a last resort.[3]

There was also interest in what could be called facilitated DPOs in which an underwriter played a role in helping companies use the internet to attract investors. In June 1997 the Australian Stock Exchange announced plans to set up a market on the Internet for small- and medium-sized firms to raise capital.[4] However this plan was not successful. Also, the founders of Spring Street Brewing subsequently founded Wit Capital to serve as an underwriter of internet offerings. In 2000 Wit Capital co-managed 57 offerings and was involved in 71 other deals. E-Offering, established by the brokerage firm E-trade led 8 deals. Also in 2000, E-Trade sold E-Offering to Wit Capital.[5]

---

[1] http://www.inc.com/magazine/19990901/13720.html

[2] http://www.va-interactive.com/inbusiness/editorial/finance/articles/offerings.html

[3] Two firms that once had internet data available but whose sites no longer work are: Direct IPO (http://www.directipo.com/), a consulting and publishing service that helps technology companies raise capital through the internet, and Nikko Investor, an investor relations company that provided information on internet IPOs in Japan at (http://www.nikkoir.co.jp/sinki-e/sinki-e.htm).

[4] Australian Stock Exchange plans Internet market for smaller firms, Asian Wall Street Journal, June 12, 1997, p. 22. However, it appears that these plans never materialized.

[5] http://www.thestandard.com/wit-capital-gets-focused.

There continues to be interest in direct IPOs. In 2009 Cambridge Financial Services advertised the ability to help with direct IPOs.[1] In September 2008 E = MC[2] Company, Inc. began a private placement offering to sell up to 5 million USD of convertible preferred stock via the internet. The company intends to establish the Green Stock Exchange to traded shares of green companies.[2]

3.4. Important events in the IPO aftermarket

3.4.1. Syndicate short positions and stabilization bids

Aggarwal (2000) examines 114 IPOS and reports that the syndicate typically starts out with a short position, which averages 17.08 percent of the offering. This short position occurs because the underwriter sells more shares to investors at the offering price than it buys from the issuer. A standard part of the underwriter's contract with the issuer provides a **Greenshoe option** that allows the underwriter to purchase up to an additional 15% of the shares offered for 30 days after the offering.[3] Hence, the first 15 percentage points of the syndicate's initial short position are covered by this option. If the price of the IPO increases from the offering price, the Greenshoe option is exercised and the initial short position is eliminated. If the price declines, the underwriter covers the short position by purchasing shares in the secondary market.[4] Aftermarket short covering is concentrated in the first few days after the offering. Aggarwal (2000) reports that 61 (53.5%) of her IPO sample experienced short covering in the aftermarket. Of these, all had short covering on the day after the

---

In 2000 Wit merged with SoundView Technology Group, which, in turn, was acquired by Charles Schwab in 2003.
http://en.wikipedia.org/wiki/SoundView_Technology_Group

[1] http://www.cfss.com/direct-ipo.html

[2] http://greensx.com/info/aboutus.php

[3] The term comes from Green Shoe Manufacturing, which was the first underwriting contract to contain this provision.

[4] Ellis, Michaely, and O'Hara (2000) document the role of the lead underwriter in the aftermarket.

offering, but less than 20% were still experiencing short covering 20 days after the offering.

Underwriters can place **stabilization bids** to support the IPO stock price in the aftermarket, but these bids must be flagged so that they are transparent and must be at the offer price or less. Aggarwal (2000) reports no instances of the use of stabilization bids.

3.4.2. Short selling by traders

Without sellers aftermarket trading of IPOs cannot begin. **Flipping**, which is the sale of stock purchased from the underwriter, provides one source of aftermarket supply. Aggarwal (2003) reports that during the first two days of aftermarket trading, flippers account for only 19 percent of trading volume. Short sellers provide another source of supply in the IPO aftermarket. Short sellers can generally borrow stock to facilitate short selling even on the first trading day except in the smallest issues.[1]

3.4.3. Penalty bids

For many IPOs the underwriter or syndicate members post a penalty bid, which is an offer to buy back the shares sold in the offering. Syndicate members typically lose their internal syndicate commission if the syndicate has to buy the stock back in the aftermarket. The penalty bid is generally in effect for 30 calendar days.

3.4.4. Quiet period

The U.S. Securities and Exchange Commission mandates a 25-calendar-day quiet period during which comments from underwriters and the issuer are prohibited. All relevant information should be provided in the registration statement so there should be no need to make additional comments about a firm or its prospects until sufficient time has passed that updates are needed. However, there is no quiet period in some countries such as Australia.

---

[1] Geczy, Musto, and Reed (2002).

3.4.5. Rule 144, Rule 701 and lockup

Under SEC Rule 144 individuals such as officers and directors of U.S. firms who hold unregistered shares can begin to sell these shares subject to the limitations set forth in the rule. Moreover, U.S. SEC Rule 701 permits non-affiliates to sell shares acquired prior to the offering beginning 90 days after the offering date.[1] However, underwriters often insist on a **lockup**, a contract between large investors and the underwriter prohibiting the sale of stock in the aftermarket, typically for 180 days. However, if the trading in the aftermarket is going well the underwriter sometimes releases individuals or institutions from the lockup requirements, which accounts for the fact that 15% of IPOs have insider sales prior to lockup expiration.[2]

4. Rights offerings

A **rights offering** is used to raise equity by selling additional shares of common stock to a firm's current shareholders.[3] Selling new equity via a rights offering is generally cheaper than using a firm commitment underwriting. Rights offerings are common in Japan and in the UK and its former colonies such as Australia, Singapore, and India. However, rights offerings are seldom used in the U.S.

In most cases each shareholders receives one right for each share held. Once the rights are distributed they are often traded on in the secondary market. However, sometimes the shareholder will receive multiple rights per share. Shareholders who receive rights they do not want to exercise can usually sell them. Rights entitle the holder to purchase shares of a firm's common stock at a stated price prior to the expiration of the right. Rights have a very short life so that funds are received by the firm very quickly and there is not much time for the stock's price to decline below the exercise price. The exercise price is lower than the market price at the time the right is issued. The rights offering will not be successful if the market price of the

---

[1] Bradley, Jordan, and Yi (2001).

[2] Brav and Gompers (2003).

[3]See http://thismatter.com/money/stocks/rights-offering.htm for an excellent description of right offerings. The site also describes an actual rights offering.

firm's stock falls below the exercise price. Many firms enter into a **standby commitment** in which an investment bank agrees to purchase any shares not bought by current shareholders and to resell these shares to clients.

Investors face two questions about rights: What is the value of a right? What is the theoretical price of the stock after the rights offering? These questions can be answered by examining an individual portfolio or the firm as a whole. Modigliani and Miller's proposition 1, which states that the value of a firm is invariant to its capital structure, is the basis for answering these two questions. According to this proposition, a rights offering will only increase the value of a firm by the amount of funds raised in the rights offering. Two examples will show how to answer these two questions. A third example describes an actual rights offering.

Example 1. Suppose that the current price of a firm's common stock is 10 USD and that an investor owns 90 shares. Prior to the rights offering, the investor's portfolio is worth (10 USD X 90 shares =) 900 USD. This firm distributes rights entitling the owner to purchase one share of its common stock at a price of 8 USD for each share owned now. Upon exercising the rights the investor will give the firm 720 USD and receive 90 shares. So after the rights offering the investor will own 180 shares worth (900 USD + 720 USD =) 1,620 USD. Hence, each share will be worth (1,620 USD/180) = 9 USD; this is the theoretical price of a share of stock after the rights offering. Note that one right entitles the holder to purchase one share of stock that will be worth 9 USD by paying 8 USD. Hence, the right is worth 1 USD.

Example 2. The current price of a firm's common stock is 10 USD and an investor owns 90 shares of the firm's stock. Prior to the rights offering, the portfolio is worth (10 USD X 90 shares =) 900 USD. This firm distributes rights entitling the owner to purchase one share of its common stock at a price of 8 USD for each three rights. To exercise the rights the investor will give the firm (90/3 X 8 USD) = 240 USD and receive 30 shares. So after the rights offering the investor will own 120 shares worth (900 USD + 240 USD =) 1,140 USD. Hence, each share will be worth (1,140 USD/120) = 9.50 USD; this is the theoretical price of a share of stock after the rights offering. Note that three rights entitle the holder to purchase one share of stock that will be worth 9.50 USD by paying 8 USD. Hence, each right is worth (9.50 USD – 8 USD)/3 = 0.50 USD.

Example 3. In July 2010, Hanmi Financial Corporation distributed right allowing shareholders to purchase 1 new share for each share currently owned. The purchase exercise price of the rights was 1.20 USD per share. The company announced the successful completion of its rights offering on July 27, 2010. On July 26, 2010 the firm's stock price closed at 1.24 USD.[1]

5. Auctions

Auctions are used to sell equities, and, especially, fixed-income securities. U.S. government debt, the debt of U.S states and their subdivisions, and some issues of utility companies are sold by auction. Other governments such as Singapore also use auctions to sell debt. In Chile IPOs are sold by brokers using a special stock exchange auction session. These auction sessions were a popular way for state enterprises involved in privatizations to sell their shares to the public. Since there are no underwriters, there is no underwriting spread. Instead, brokers charge commissions. French companies can also use an auction procedure described below. In the 1990s in Japan 50% or more of the shares of each issue were offered by auction and the remaining shares were sold at a price based on the auction price.[2] We turn to a more detailed examination of auctions for equities and debt.

5.1. Equities

On 19 August 2004 Google sold about 19.6 million shares at 85 USD each using a Dutch auction. Two additional firms using this method are Overstock.com and RedEnvelope.

Figure 1-1 illustrates a Dutch auction. Suppose that a company plans to sell 5 million shares in an IPO using a Dutch auction. A hypothetical example shows how such an auction works. Suppose that six investors submit bids for a total of 5.1 million shares. The company arranges the bids from highest to lowest. Note that the first five bidders together are offering to purchase all of the shares being offered. Further, bidders 1-4 are offering

---

[1] http://www.marketwatch.com/story/hanmi-financial-corporation-announces-successful-closing-of-offerings-2010-07-27?reflink=MW_news_stmp

[2] For a description of the Japanese system see Pettway and Kaneko (1996).

to pay more than bidder 5, so these bidders will receive all of the shares that they are seeking and bidder 5 will receive the shares that are left after satisfying the demand of bidders 1-4. Given the bids shown, bidder 5 will receive 1 million shares. Typically, all successful bidders will pay the price of the successful bidder biding the lowest price. In our example, all bidders pay 26 USD. If all bidders pay the price that they actually bid, rather than the lowest price, the auction is a **Yankee auction.**

Figure 1-1. Illustration of a Dutch auction

Investor	Bid in USD	Number of shares	
	(per share)	Sought	Remaining
1	1,000.00	5,000	4,995,000
2	50.00	1,000,000	3,995,000
3	31.76	595,000	3,400,000
4	28.00	2,400,000	1,000,000
5	26.00	1,100,000	-100,000
6	23.01	200,000	0

In France both the bookbuilding and fixed price IPO methods are used, but a unique auction method, called **Offre à Prix Minimal**, is also used. One purpose of the auction is to encourage investors to reveal their true assessment of the value of the shares. Typically, about one week before the offering the underwriter and issuer set a minimum acceptable price. Then, on the day before the IPO is to begin trading investors submit confidential price and quantity bids. After receiving the bids, the Société des Bourses Françaises calculates a cumulative demand curve. The issuer, underwriter, and the market regulator then negotiate the offering price and a maximum allowable bid price. Bids above the maximum allowable price are disqualified. The purpose of this procedure is to discourage bids that are unrealistic and do not truly reflect the assessment of the investor as to the value of the securities. All investors who have made bids between the selected price and the maximum allowable bid price receive shares. If the offer is oversubscribed shares are allocated on a pro rata basis. If the ratio of demand to supply is very high, say over 20 times, then the offer can be postponed and converted to a fixed price offering. This happened 20 times out of 99 Offre à Prix Minimal offerings from 1992 through 1998.

5.2. Bonds

5.2.1. U.S. Treasury securities

Like many countries the U.S. sells its debt via public auction. In 2008 there were more than 250 auctions of these securities with a value of 6.7 trillion USD. The auctions are announced and bids are solicited. Institutions submit competitive bids indicating the yield they are seeking. Noncompetitive bids for 5 million USD or less of bonds can be submitted by individuals and smaller institutions. These bidders agree to accept the rate determined in the competitive auction. When the auction ends, the U.S. accepts all noncompetitive bids. Competitive bids are accepted starting with the lowest yield and continuing with successively higher yields until the quantity offered equals the quantity bought.. In U.S. Treasury auctions, all buyers receive the same rate, which is the rate paid to the bidder bidding the highest rate actually accepted.

5.2.2. U.S. municipal bonds

In this section we describe how municipal bonds are issued. The characteristics of municipal bonds are described in a subsequent chapter.

Many municipalities in the U.S. sell their bonds in auctions through competitive bidding. The issuer or its adviser prepares an offering statement describing the bonds to be sold, distributes the statement to potential buyers such as investment bankers, and establishes a deadline for bids. Bidders submit their bids, typically just prior to the deadline. Often, the bid is stated in terms of **net interest cost**, which is defined as N/D where N is the sum of the non-discounted sum of the total future interest payments plus any discount and minus any premium and D is total bond years. To calculate D begin by calculating for any year in which there is a maturity of principal the product of amount of principal maturing times the number of years to maturity. Total bond years are the sum of that product for all years in which there is a principal maturity. When the bids are opened, the bonds are sold to the lowest bidder. If the winning bidder is an investment banker, the bonds are typically resold to the firm's customers.

In a negotiated sale the bonds are sold to an investment banker or institution at a price that is negotiated between the two parties. This method may be preferable for sellers with little experience or with bond sizes that are unlikely to attract bidders. However, academic research generally shows that the interest rates paid by sellers using competitive bidding are substantially lower than interest rates for bonds sold through negotiated sales, especially for issues that attract many bidders.[1]

6. Short selling

Short selling is surprisingly common, representing 24% of NYSE and 31% of NASDAQ share volume.[2] Further, short sellers often correctly predict future negative abnormal returns. Hence, all traders need to be familiar with short selling.

Short selling involves the selling of stock not owned. Typically, after the sale, the seller's broker borrows stock to deliver to the purchaser. Thus, the short seller's counterparty, i.e., the buyer, is the registered owner of the stock with all voting rights, rights to dividends and so forth. The lender can demand return of the shares at any time. If the short seller is not able to find a replacement lender, the short sale must be closed out by purchasing shares and returning them to the lender. However, recalls are rare. The short seller is responsible for paying any dividends that the lender misses by not being the registered owner on the dividend record date. The short seller gives the proceeds of the sale to the lender as collateral. The lender invests these funds in U.S. Treasury securities and rebates any earnings in excess of the loan fees to the borrower. The portion of the earnings returned is the **rebate rate.** Most lenders are institutions, but in some countries such as Singapore and the U.S. individuals can lend stock.[3]

A **naked short** sale occurs when a trader sells stock short without any intension of borrowing the stock. A naked short sale results in a **fail to deliver**. One reason that brokers may engage in a naked short sale is to avoid paying when costs of borrowing are high. Active traders and market

---

[1] Simonsen and Robbins (1996).

[2] Diether, Lee, and Werner (2009).

[3] http://www.cdp.com.sg/business/lend.html

makers may sell a stock on one day and buy it back quickly, but on a subsequent day. Knowing that the fail to deliver will be automatically cleared on the settlement day of the stock purchase, the traders may decide to do nothing.

Naked short selling was widely criticized during the market crash of 2008 and many countries banned it. Critics argued that naked short selling allowed traders to drive the price of stock down during periods of market stress. In addition to banning naked short selling, the U.S. adopted a **locate rule,** which requires that a short seller locate shares to borrow prior to making a short sale. However, despite this rule a fail to deliver can still occur because multiple short sellers may identify the same stock as available for borrowing. A **Threshold Security List** was established to identify stocks with at least 10,000 shares with fail to deliver status for five consecutive settlement days. Brokers are required to make delivery within 13 days if a stock is on the Threshold Security List.

D'Avolio (2002) studies borrowing and lending using data from a large U.S. institution. He reports that the average stock is easy to borrow since only 7% of the loan supply is borrowed. The cost for these stocks is 25 basis points per year. About 10% of stocks are never borrowed, which means they are never shorted; these are mostly small illiquid stocks. Stocks that are difficult to borrow and, consequently, have high loan fees are called **special**. 9% of stocks were found to be special, having loan fees above 1%. The mean loan fee for these stocks was 4.3% per year. **Specialness** refers to the difference between the typical rebate rate and the rebate rate on a given loan.

IPOs can generally be borrowed, but are almost always special. Specialness generally decreases with a stock's **float**. Only a few stocks (seven per month on average) were found to be extremely special, requiring negative rebates. **Negative rebates** occur when the loan fee exceeds the risk free rate so that the lender retains all the earnings from investing the proceeds and also demands additional fees from the borrower. Such a security is in high demand relative to the stock available for lending and, hence, the lender is able to retain a larger portion of the earnings from investing the proceeds of the short sale. Stock loan rates are not usually re-priced during their life so a lender may recall a loan if the interest rates change during the life of the loan.

Not all short sellers seek to profit from a stock's price decline. In a **short sale against the box** the seller actually owns shares, but the shares are not readily available for delivery. The owner sells short and later covers when the shares become available. Other short sellers may be long one stock and short another, hoping that the price of the shorted stock will fall relative to the price of the long stock. However, such a change in the relative prices can occur even if both prices go up. Market professionals and market makers may short stock to accommodate investor demands.

Through short selling investors create claims on equities and fixed-income securities. Consider two investors, A and B, who initially have no ownership positions in the stock of International Business Machines, along with a third investor, C, who owns 100 shares of IBM. B's broker enters into a contract with C in which B borrows C's 100 shares of IBM. B agrees to return C's shares whenever C requires and promises to reimburse C for any dividends that are paid on IMB while the shares are borrowed. B also pays C a fee as an inducement for entering into the contract. B then sells 100 shares of IMB to A on the floor of the NYSE. B's broker delivers C's shares to A's broker in return for the sales proceeds. The sales proceeds are typically given to C or C's broker as collateral. If IBM's price increases additional collateral may be required. Depending on the results of the negotiating process, C may retain any interest earned on the funds deposited as collateral or may share the interest with B or B's broker. In this situation A is in exactly the same position that would arise from a normal purchase of IBM while B is in an opposite position which is similar to that of the issuing firm.[1] When the short position is closed, B purchases shares on the floor of the NYSE and returns the shares to C in return for the collateral. If the repurchase price plus commissions and dividends is less than the original sale price, B has a profit. Otherwise B has a loss.[2]

---

[1] However, the borrower gets to vote the shares and the payments that the lender receives in lieu of dividends do not receive any favorable tax treatment.

[2] If shares sold short represent 1% of the firm's shares, long investors own claims that are identical to 101% of IBM and short investors owe claims to 1% of IBM.

The International Securities Lending Association is a trade association of institutions that lend their stock. The Association's web site provides example of lending agreements and other information about securities lending.[1]

Historically, many markets have placed limits on the execution of short sales. One such restriction that was in place in the U.S. from 1938 to 2007 was the uptick rule. An **uptick** is a trade price higher than the last trade price, a **zero tick** is a trade price equal to the last trade price, and a **downtick** is a trade price lower that the last trade price. A **zero-plus tick** is a price that is the same as the last price, but higher than the last different price. The uptick rule required that a short sale could only be made on an uptick or zero-plus tick.

One objective of short sellers may be to profit from a decline in the price of the assets sold short. In this case the investor attempts to sell the shares and repurchase them subsequently at a lower price. Short selling benefits financial markets if it moves prices to equilibrium values more quickly than would be the case without short selling. In fact, without short selling investors who do not own a stock cannot easily take advantage of a view that a stock is overpriced. Despite these potential benefits short selling is generally not popular with company management. Short sellers necessarily have a negative view of the prospects for the firm and sometimes even spread rumors about adverse developments. Short selling tends to depress stock prices initially, though the evidence shows that in general short selling does not materially affect prices. In fact, short sellers increase liquidity.

In the U.S. in the past short selling has been associated with various types of stock price manipulation. In some cases syndicates have been formed that would sell large amounts of a firm's stock short and then buy back later when public selling drove the price even lower. This strategy can backfire. Consider a case in which a single individual simultaneously purchases shares and lends these shares to short sellers. Eventually the individual owns more than 100% of the firm's stock. Then, the lender demands the return of shares from the borrowers/short sellers. However, the short sellers can only buy shares to return from the lender because the lender owns all of the real shares. The owner/lender can demand a high price from the short

---

[1] http://www.isla.co.uk/

sellers forcing them to incur large losses. In these cases a regulator may step in and force the lender to sell shares. These types of incidents have lead some countries to prohibit short selling entirely and others to prohibit certain types of investors such as individuals from selling short.[1]

7. Summary

This chapter discusses the primary market, which is the market for selling new securities to raise funds for businesses and governments. The securities can be sold to a small group of investors in a private placement or to a large group of investors in a public offering. The public offering leads to the creation of secondary markets for these securities, which we discuss in the next chapter. Public offerings can be accomplished by underwriters using the fixed price or bookbuild methods, by best efforts underwritings, by auctions, by direct offerings over the Internet, and by rights offerings. All of these methods are currently in use, indicating that each method is appropriate in particular circumstances.

Questions

1. Why are auctions more commonly used for selling government debt than new equity?
2. Why do you think that direct public offerings have not been very successful?
3. Since rights offerings are cheaper than other ways of raising new equity capital, why do many firms prefer these other methods?
4. Which method of raising new equity would likely have the greatest effect on the value of a firm, a private placement or an IPO?
5. Compare the advantages and disadvantages of private placements and public offerings.

References

Aggarwal, Reena, 2000, Allocation of initial public offerings and flipping activity, Journal of Financial Economics 68, 111-135.

---

[1] A number of these incidents are discussed in Walker (1991).

Arugaslan, Onur, Douglas O. Cook, and Robert Kieschnick, 2005, Monitoring as a motivation for IPO underpricing, Journal of Finance 59, 2403-2420.

Australian Stock Exchange plans Internet market for smaller firms, Asian Wall Street Journal, June 12, 1997, p. 22.

Balachandran, Balasingham, Robert Faff, and Michael Theobald, 2008, Rights offerings, takeup, renounceability, and underwriting status, Journal of Financial Economics 89, 328-346.

Benveniste, Lawrence M. and Walid Y. Busaba, 1997, Bookbuilding vs. fixed price: an analysis of competing strategies for marketing IPOs, Journal of Financial and Quantitative Analysis 32, 383-403.

Brav, Alon and Paul A. Gompers, 2003, The role of lockups in initial public offerings, Review of Financial Studies 16, 1-29.

Carey, Mark; Steven Prowse, John Rea, and Gregory F. Udell, 1993, The economics of private placements: A new look. Financial Markets, Institutions and Instruments 2, 1-67.

D'Avolio, Gene, 2002, The market for borrowing stock, Journal of Financial Economics 66, 271-306.

Diether, K., K-H. Lee, and I. Werner, 2009, Short-sale strategies and return predictability, Review of Financial Studies 22, 575-607.

Ellis, Katrina, Roni Michaely, and Maureen O'Hara, 2002, When the underwriter is the market maker: an examination of trading in the IPO aftermarket, Journal of Finance 55, 1039-1074.

Geczy, Christopher C., David K. Musto, and Adam V. Reed, 2002, Stocks are special too: an analysis of the equity lending market, Journal of Financial Economics 66, 241-269.

Handley, K.W., 1993, The underpricing of initial public offerings and the partial adjustments phenomenon, Journal of Financial Economics 34, 231-250.

Jain, Archana, Pankaj K. Jain, Thomas H. McInish, and Michael McKenzie, 2013, Worldwide reach of short selling regulations, Journal of Financial Economics 109, 177-197.

Pettway, R. H. and T. Kaneko, 1996, The effects of removing price limits and introducing auctions upon short-term IPO returns: The case of Japanese IPOs, Pacific-Basin Finance Journal 4, 241-258.

Saffi, Pedro A., and Kari Sigurdsson, 2011, Price Efficiency and short selling, Review of Financial Studies 24, 821-852.

Sherman, Ann Guenther, 1992, The pricing of best efforts new issues, Journal of Finance 47, 781-790.

Simonsen, William and Mark D. Robbins, 1996, Does it make any difference anymore? Competitive versus negotiated municipal bond issuance, Public Administration Review 56, 57-64.

Sjostrom, William K., Jr., 2001, Going public through an Internet direct public offering: A sensible alternative for small companies? Florida Law Review 53, 529-566.

Woolridge, J. Randall and Amy Dickinson, 1994, Short selling and common stock prices, Financial Analysts Journal 50, 20-28.

CHAPTER TWO

SECONDARY MARKETS

Key Terms

Adverse information costs—the costs incurred or anticipated by a dealer as a result of trading with counterparties who are motivated by the possession of superior insight into the appropriate equilibrium price of the asset.

Algorithmic trading—trading where decisions are made by a computer.

Ask—the sale price set by a trader or market maker.

Asymmetric information costs—the component of the spread arising from different information between liquidity suppliers and demanders. See adverse information costs.

Batch trade— See call trade.

BBO—the best bid offer.

Benchmark exception (to the Order Protection Rule)—a U.S. Securities and Exchange Commission rule allowing an exchange to execute at a price inferior to the current NBBO as long as the execution price equals the benchmark price.

Benchmark price—a price equal to or better than the least aggressive (worst) NBBO quoted over the last one second.

Best bid offer (BBO)—the best bid and ask currently available in the market.

Buy-side—institutional investors such as pension funds, mutual funds, and hedge funds that are clients of brokers.

Call trade—trades for which orders are accumulated, the market is opened, trades for which counterparties can agree on a price are executed, and the market is closed.

Co-locate—locating non-exchange computers near to exchange computers.

Consolidated Quotation System (**CQS**)—the electronic service that provides quotation information for exchanges and ECNs.

Consolidated Tape System (CTS)—The overall organization responsible for the Consolidated Quotation System and the Consolidated Trade System.

Consolidated Trade System—the electronic service that disseminates information on each trade for exchanges and ECNs.

Continuous market—a market that permits counterparties to trade with each other whenever they can agree on a price.

Crossing networks—firms that collect orders from institutions and periodically conduct a batch trade.

Dark market or pool—a market that is not displaying quotes.

Dealer markets—a market in which liquidity is supplied by professionals.

Depth—the number of shares available at a given price or in aggregate.

Direct market access—clients of a brokerage firm can interact directly with the order book of an exchange.

ECN—see electronic communication network.

Effective spread—the signed difference between the midpoint of the BBO and the trade price.

Electronic Communication Networks (ECN)—computer systems for trading securities outside an exchange.

Exchange—an organization whose members or participants trade securities among themselves at a fixed location, which can be either a computer or a trading floor.

High frequency trading or trader (HFT)—the use of computers to make and execute trading decisions, entering, executing or canceling orders often within milliseconds.

Frontrunning—trading ahead of client orders by brokers.

Good today—an order designation indicating that the order expires at the end of trading for the day if it has not been executed.

Good until cancelled—an order designation indicating that an order will not expire except as required by exchange rules.

Hidden orders—limit orders that do not affect the displayed quote of depth.

High-frequency trading—a type of algorithmic trading in which computers are used to make and place orders to trade.

Iceberg orders—limit orders that are divided into a visible part displayed to the market and the remainder that is not visible. When the visible part is executed additional shares are made visible to keep the visible part at its initial size.

Intermarket sweep order—an order to be executed on the exchange to which it is sent regardless of whether the exchange is quoting at the NBBO.

Inventory holding costs—the costs incurred or anticipated by a dealer as a result of inventory positions acquired in the process of market making.

Latency—the speed at which trading venues or traders are able to communicate.

Limit order book—a stock of unexecuted limit orders.

Limit order—an order to be executed at a specified price or better.

Liquidity demand—orders demanding immediate execution.

Liquidity supply—orders that are available as counterparties to trades demanding liquidity.

Liquidity—the ability to buy or sell an asset at a price close to its current market price.

Listed—a security has been approved for trading on an exchange and meets the exchange's requirements.

Lit market—a market that delivers its best bid and offer to the consolidated tape.

Maker/taker pricing—providers of liquidity (makers) receive a credit from the trading venue and demanders of liquidity (takers) pay a fee. In rare cases the payer and receiver roles are reversed.

Making a market—always willing to buy or sell at a price close to the current market price.

Market architecture—the institutional arrangements for trading in a market.

Market microstructure—the study of the way financial markets are organized and how that organization affects risk, liquidity, market efficiency, market integrity, transactions costs, and any other aspects of markets.

Market order—an order to buy or sell immediately at the best possible price.

Marketable limit order—a limit order with a limit price that can be immediately executed.

Minimum trading unit—the smallest permitted unit of trading.

MTF—see multilateral trading facility.

Multilateral Trading Facility (MTF)—The European Union's version of an ECN.

National Best Bid Offer (NBBO)—the best bid and offer considering all exchanges quoting a particular security.

Odd lot—less than the usual unit of trading.

Order—instructions to buy or sell an asset.

Open outcry—a method of trading in which traders stand so that they can see each other and call out their bids and asks.

Order designation—instructions about how to handle an order.

Order driven—a type of trading in which liquidity is supplied by market participants, typically through a limit order book.

Order processing costs—the costs associated with supplying liquidity such as the cost of equipment and employees.

Order Protection Rule—an exchange receiving an order, but not quoting the NBBO cannot execute the order, but must forward the order to an exchange that is quoting the NBBO unless an exception applies. This is U.S. Securities and Exchange Commission rule 611.

Over-the-counter—not traded on an exchange. Most fixed-income securities and foreign exchange trades are over the counter.

Pairs trading—Buying one stock and shorting another to take advantage of perceived mispricing.

Picking off risk—the risk that an informed party will take advantage of a price offered by a liquidity supplier.

Pit—a trading location on a futures exchange that typically comprises stairs depressed below floor level.

Post-trade transparency—the information provided to the market by a trading venue after a trade.

Precedence—a marketplace's rules about which trades come first.

Pre-trade transparency—the information provided to the market by a trading venue prior to a trade.

Price discovery—the identification of the equilibrium price of an asset through trading.

Price priority—a rule that orders at a better price are executed before orders at inferior prices.

Quote driven—a market is which dealers supply liquidity.

Quoted spread—the difference between the best bid and the best ask.

Realized spread—the signed difference between the trade price and the midpoint of the BBO at a specified time following the trade.

Resiliency—the speed with which depth on the limit order book is replenished after a trade.

Round lot—the usual unit of trading.

Round trip—the purchase and sale of an asset.

Scale order—the simultaneous entry of limit orders at multiple prices, either below the current price for a buy or above for a sell.

Secondary market—a market for trading securities among owners that does not involve the issuer of the securities.

Sell-side—brokers and investment bankers.

Spread—the difference between the ask and bid.

Stale price—reflects out of date information or a price that the informed traders know does not reflect the stock's true value.

Statistical arbitrage—determining which of a pair of assets is overvalued and undervalued based on past price relationships.

Stop loss order—a stop order to sell.

Stop order—an order that is held for execution if the asset price trades at or beyond a stated limit.

Stop-limit—a stop order that become a limit order when an asset trades at or beyond a specified price.

Stop-market—a stop order that become a market order when the asset trades at or beyond a specified price.

Thick—a liquid market.

Thin—an illiquid market.

Tick size—the minimum allowable price variation.

Time precedence—a rule that orders are executed in the order received.

Trade Reporting Facility (TRF)—an electronic arrangement for reporting trade price and volume for trades that take place off an exchange.

Trade through—a trade at a price that is inferior to a price available from another trader or market.

Trailing stop—a stop order that becomes a market order if an asset's price declines by a fixed amount (either in money or in percent) from its most recent high.

Transparency—the amount of information available to the market.

Walk down the limit order book—execution of a sell order at increasingly lower prices on the limit order book.

Walk up the limit order book—execution of a buy order at increasingly higher prices on the limit order book.

IN THIS CHAPTER, we discuss the secondary market in which securities are traded among investors. Specifically, we examine the benefits of these markets including

- Providing liquidity, and
- Allowing price discovery.

Next, we consider issues related to trading, including

- The types of orders to buy or sell that can be used,
- Designations that can be used to modify how orders are handled,
- More sophisticated types of orders,
- Minimum tick sizes and spreads,
- Round lots and odd lots, and
- The order in which trades are executed.

Then we turn our attention to ways of trading, namely:

- Dealer markets,
- Limit order books,
- Call markets, and
- Open outcry.

Finally, we consider trading venues:

- Exchanges,
- Alternative Trading Systems such as
    - Crossing networks, and
    - Electronic Communication Networks (ECNs)
- Over-the-counter

1. Introduction

A **secondary market** is a market for trading assets among investors. Equities, fixed income securities, foreign exchange, and derivatives are all traded in secondary markets. The specific rules and institutions for trading these four product types are collectively called **market architecture.** The details of market architecture differ from market to market, but from a broader perspective, there are only a few ways of organizing secondary markets. We consider the major ways of trading in secondary markets. There has been an explosion of interest in understanding secondary markets, leading to a new field of study—market microstructure. **Market microstructure** is the study of the way financial markets are organized and how that organization affects risk, liquidity, market efficiency, market integrity, transactions costs, and any other aspects of markets. Hundreds of scholars and practitioners now devote their careers to the study of market microstructure and the application of its precepts.

The aggregate value of equity for companies traded on exchanges worldwide increased from 8,893 trillion USD in 1990 to 49,146 trillion USD in 2009. This increase in value was the result of increasing stock prices over the period, growth in the number of firms with equity trading on exchange, and growth in the number of countries with exchanges. There was also growth in the value of other financial assets over this period. In 2007 the total value of global financial assets reached 194 trillion USD, but the world-wide economic recession reduced these values in subsequent years.[1]

2. Benefits of secondary markets

2.1. Liquidity

Liquidity is the ability to buy or sell an asset at a price close to its current market price. Liquid markets are **thick** and illiquid markets are **thin**. Liquidity is one of the most important benefits of a secondary market because more liquid assets command a higher price, which reduces the cost of capital. More than 40 years ago the U.S. government studied the discounts that were necessary to sell restricted common stock and the findings of this study are as relevant today as they were then. At the time restricted stock could not be resold for two years. Table 2-1, which presents the results of the study, shows that for large issues of 100 million USD or more only 7 out of 24 issues required a discount of less than 20 percent and 2 issues actually required a discount of more than 40 percent. For the 66 very small issues of less than 100,000 USD, 18 required discounts of more than 40%.

---

1 http://www.mckinsey.com/mgi/publications/gcm_sixth_annual_report/executive_summary.asp

Table 2-1. Discounts on purchase price of restricted common stock classified by size of transaction and sales of issuer, January 1, 1966 to June 30, 1969 (Publicly Held Companies Only)

Sales of Issuer	No	USD
Panel A: Discounts >= 40.1%		
Less than 100	18	5,449
100-999	9	1,695
1,000-4,999	21	12,777
5,000-19,999	10	2,767
20,000-99,999	6	4,979
100,000 or More	2	1,805
Total	66	29,471
Panel B: Discount 20.1% to 40.0%		
Less than 100	33	31,839
100-999	1	500
1,000-4,999	27	20,541
5,000-19,999	38	535224
20,000-99,999	14	23,317
100,000 or More	5	9,954
Total	118	139,376
Panel C: Discount 0.1% to 20.0%		
Less than 100	15	24,833
100-999	3	4,897
1,000-4,999	13	11,647
5,000-19,999	71	34,191
20,000-99,999	35	58,714
100,000 or More	17	35,792
Total	154	170,074

Note: USD amounts in thousands.

Source: Discounts involved in purchases of common stock, in U.S. 92d Congress, 1st Session. House: Institutional Investor Study Report of the Securities and Exchange Commission, Washington, D.C.: U.S. Government Print Off. (March 10, 1971), 5:2444-2456. (Document No. 92-64, Part 5)

Lower liquidity results in higher trading costs that are incurred every time the asset is bought and sold. If two assets are identical except that one has a cost of liquidity that is 100 basis point higher than the other, investors demand an additional monthly return of 0.21% for the higher-cost asset.[1]

Using an interesting options approach to determine the value of liquidity, Longstaff (1995) presents even more surprising results. For high volatility securities, a 1-day restriction on marketability can result in a discount of 1.268 percent and a 5 year restriction can result in a discount of about 66 percent. Hence, for high volatility assets the removal of a five year restriction on trading the asset would triple its value.

2.2. Price discovery

Financial markets also facilitate **price discovery,** the identification of the equilibrium price of an asset through trading. In addition to traders, price discovery benefits firms issuing stock by revealing the market's assessment of the value of the firm's investments. A firm's share price is a crucial determinant of the firm's cost of capital and also helps in understanding the riskiness of the firm. Competitors or potential competitors may benefit from learning about attractive new markets. Issuers of government debt learn the market's assessment of the soundness of their fiscal policies.

The same security may trade in many markets. Also, many different types of investors trade the same security. There is widespread interest in determining which markets and which market participants first incorporate new information into trading prices. How this incorporation of information is affected by market architecture is also of interest. Scholars have developed three major technologies for identifying which markets or market participants contribute to price discovery. Each technique focuses on a different aspect of price discovery. We begin by grouping trades for a given stock by trader type. Harris, McInish, and Wood (2002) call these groups channels. Harris, McInish and Wood (2002) focus on which channel error corrects to the other, or, alternately, which channel avoids chasing spurious trends. Hasbrouck (1995) focuses on a market's information share, which is the proportion of the efficient price innovation attributable to that

---

[1] Amihud and Mendelson (1988).

market. Barclay and Warner (1993, 2003) focus on the weighted contribution of each channel to price change over time. Barclay and Warner's approach is the only one of the three that does not require sophisticated econometrics.

3. Trading particulars

3.1. Order types

An investor wanting to buy or sell a security must give a broker an **order** that gives instructions to buy or sell an asset. With the proliferation of computerized trading systems, the variety of orders that can be used has mushroomed. Before considering more sophisticated orders, we describe the three most common orders.

Market orders: A **market order** is an order to buy or sell immediately at the best possible price. A trader placing a market order has no guarantee concerning the execution price so this type of order is not suitable for a thin market.

Limit orders: A **limit order** is to be executed at a specified price or better. A limit order that is executed immediately either fully or in part is called a **marketable limit order**. In many cases marketable limit orders may be preferable to market orders because the trader can be sure that a trade will not occur at a price inferior to the specified price.

Stop orders: A **stop order** is an order that is held for execution if the asset price trades at or beyond a stated limit. A sell stop order has a stated limit that is lower than the current market price and this type of order is sometimes called a **stop loss order**. A stop order to buy has a stated limit that is higher than the current market price. One use of a stop order is to prevent excessive losses from a price decline for a long position or a price increase for a short position. When a stop order is activated it can be converted into a market order (**stop-market**) or a limit order (**stop-limit**). Stop orders are commonly used in futures markets, but are less common in equity markets.

Intermarket sweep orders: An intermarket sweep order is executed at the exchange to which it is sent regardless of whether that exchange is quoting at the NBBO. The initiator of an intermarket sweep order must simultaneously send an order with sufficient size to take out the top of the book depth to each exchange quoting at the NBBO. This order type is not subject to the order protection rule.

3.2. Order designations

In addition to selecting an order type, a trader may need or want to also add one or more order **designations** that provide additional details of how to handle the order. Examples of order designations are provided in Table 2-2. Because limit orders and stop orders are not likely to be executed immediately, the trader must indicate how long the order is to be in force. The two most common lengths are **good today**, which indicates that the order will expire at the end of the current trading day if not executed by then, and **good until cancelled.** Good until cancelled orders typically are in force for a number of weeks, but in most cases actually do eventually expire according to exchange rules.

3.3. Sophisticated order types

As we mentioned, with increased use of computers, more sophisticated and complicated orders are becoming common.[1] We consider a few examples. A trailing stop to sell sets the selling price at a fixed amount (either in money or in percent) below the current price, which is called the set price. Any time that the price increases above the current set price, a new set price is established. But decreases in price do not affect the set price. The process continues until either the order executes or expires. Suppose that a trader places a trailing stop at 0.03 USD, and following sequence of prices occur: 2.20, 2.21, 2.20, 2.22, 2.23, 2.24, 2.24, 2.23, 2.22, 2.21, 2.21, 2.19. The stop order would become a market order to sell when the option traded at 2.21 and if the market is thick the option would most likely have been sold at that price. A trailing stop to buy works similarly, but in an opposite direction. In 2009 hidden liquidity accounted for 12.3% of the shares traded and 17.7% of the orders executed on Nasdaq.[2]

---

[1] Interactive Brokers describes 50 order types on their web site located at: http://www.interactivebrokers.com/en/p.php?f=orderTypes

[2] https://fp7.portals.mbs.ac.uk/Portals/59/docs/Hautsch.pdf

Table 2-2. Order designations

Designation	Explanation
All or none	Execute all of the order or none
Good until cancelled	Keep the order in force until cancelled or as long as exchange rules permit
Good today	Cancel the order at the end of the trading day if not executed
Fill or kill	Execute the entire order immediately or not at all
Hidden	Do not reveal the existence of the order
Iceberg	Publicly disclose the order price, but only part of its size
Immediate or cancel	Execute the portion of the order than can be done immediately and cancel the remainder
At the close	Buy or sell just prior to the close or not at all
Percent of volume	Participate in volume at a specified rate
Not held	Instructs a market maker to use judgment in executing the order.
Participate but do not initiate	Buy or sell when counterparties appear rather than immediately

Source: Prepared by authors

A scale order involves the simultaneous entry of limit orders at multiple prices, either below the current price for a buy or above for a sell. In the second half of 2010 the Australian Securities exchange introduced several new order types, including a center point order, which can be a market order or a limit order. This order is held until counterparty submits a center point order on the opposite side of the market. Then, assuming any price limit requirements are met, the two orders cross at the midpoint of the current best bid and ask.[1]

---

[1]http://www.asx.com.au/professionals/pdf/asx_trade_new_order_types.pdf

3.4. Minimum tick sizes

The minimum price change is called the **tick size**. A limit order to buy is called a **bid** and a limit order to sell is called an **ask**. The difference between the best bid, which is the highest bid, and the best ask, which is called the **spread**. The best bid and ask taken together are sometimes called the **best bid offer** or **BBO**. There has been a trend toward setting lower tick sizes.

On the Tokyo Stock Exchange the minimum tick size ranges from 1 JPY to 100,000 JPY, depending on the stock's price. In the U.S. the minimum tick size for stocks trading on lit markets is typically 0.01 USD if the stock's price is above 1 USD.

3.5. Round lots and odd lots

A **round lot** is the usual unit of trading. An **odd lot** is less than the usual unit of trading. On the Tokyo Stock Exchange a round lot is called the **minimum trading unit** (MTU). The MTU is set by each firm and currently has the following distribution: 1 share, 56 firms; 10 shares, 8 firms; 50 shares, 9 firms; 100 shares, 564 firms; 500 shares; 40 firms; 1,000 shares , 917; and 3,000 shares, 1 firm. However, on equity exchanges in the U.S. a round lot has historically been 100 shares. Since trades on most exchanges are now executed via computer there has been a trend to make the round lot size 1 share.

3.6. Precedence

Precedence refers to a marketplace's rules about which trades come first. Most exchanges follow strict price priority. Orders at better prices are executed before orders at inferior prices. Also, typically orders are executed on a first come first served basis, which is called time priority. However, at various times there have been exceptions to both of these priority rules. In reaction to traders' assertions that speed of execution was often more important than the execution price, under some circumstances trades were allowed to trade at an inferior price on one trading platform rather than having the order sent to another market with a better price because by the time the order reached the second market its better price might no longer exist. A trade at an inferior price is called a **trade through**. In the past before computers made executions with multiple counterparties less burdensome, the NYSE matched counterparties at least in part based on minimizing the number of counterparties involved in a transaction. In the past the New York Stock Exchange gave priority to public orders rather than members' orders.

Some markets allow **hidden orders**, which do not have displayed prices or quantities. **Iceberg orders** have only a portion of an order displayed. Say an order for 5,000 shares has 100 shares displayed and 4,900 shares hidden. A market order for 1,000 shares executing against this limit order would reduce its size for 4,000 shares 100 shares displayed and 3,900 shares hidden. Hidden and iceberg orders sometimes lose time priority. Some exchanges have order types that allow for hidden orders. Unlike iceberg orders, which require the display of at least one unit of the minimum trading size, these orders are completely hidden. The Direct Edge exchange has an order type (called MidPoint Match®) that only executes at the exact midpoint of the NBBO, which gives price improvement of at least one-half cent. However, these orders are executed against other orders of the same type.

4. Ways of organizing trading

Liquidity demand comes from traders who want immediate execution. This demand is expressed through the use of market orders, marketable limit orders, or other types of orders that ultimately require immediate execution such as stop orders. For trades to occur there must also be liquidity supply. A market's architecture or design determines how liquidity supply comes about.

4.1. Dealer markets

In **dealer markets** professionals supply liquidity by making a market in the assets being traded. **Making a market** means that the dealer is willing to buy or sell at a price close to the current market price. Markets that display the quotes of dealers rather that the quotes of all buyers and sellers are called **quote driven**. The Nasdaq and foreign exchange markets are quote driven markets. Nasdaq has multiple dealers competing to supply liquidity. Many banks compete to supply liquidity in the foreign exchange market.

The **spread**, which is the difference between the ask and bid, is a source of the revenue that dealers earn from market making. The spread is the dealer's gross revenue from two trades, one on each side of the market, which is called a **round trip**. The spread has three main components: order processing costs, asymmetric information costs, and inventory holding costs. Dealers incur costs from hiring staff, purchasing equipment, paying business taxes and so forth. The dealer must expect that the spread will cover these **order processing costs**. Because a dealer can spread costs over more trades, thicker stocks have lower order processing costs as a percentage of the stock's price. Larger firms typically have more active stocks and lower order processing costs.

Further, dealers face the risk that the counterparty to a trade will be informed. An informed trader has insight or knowledge about the future price movements of the asset. Hence, because the dealer is buying (selling) when the informed trader is selling (buying), the dealer expects to lose money on these trades. Hence, the spread must also be expected to cover **asymmetric information costs**. These costs may also be called **adverse information costs**. Finally, dealers typically have either a long or short inventory position in assets in which they make markets. As the prices of these assets fluctuate dealers make money or lose money on their inventory positions. If the dealers are risk adverse, they need compensation for facing these **inventory hold costs**.

The **quoted spread** is the difference between the best bid and the best ask. In a dealer market the quoted spread can be different from the **effective spread**, which is the signed difference between the midpoint of the BBO and the trade price. The quoted spread equals the effective spread if trades are not allowed between the BBO. The **realized spread** is the signed difference between the trade price and the midpoint of the best bid and offer at a specified time following the trade. The specified time is often 30 minutes, 1 hour or the end of the trading day, depending on what is most sensible for the intended use. Suppose that a stock is being quoted 20.10 bid and 20.30 ask. A trade at 20.30 may cause the BBO to change to 20.15 bid and 20.35 ask. Then suppose that there is a trade at 20.15. In this case the effective and quoted spreads are 0.20, but the realized spread is 0.15. Realized spreads are typically smaller than effective spreads.

4.2. Limit order books

Order driven markets use trading rules to determine which trades are executed. Oral auctions and crossing networks, among others, are order driven. Some markets supply liquidity via a **limit order book**, which is the collection of limit orders that cannot be executed immediately because there are no counterparties willing to trade at the limit order price. This type of market in which all of the orders of both buyers and sellers are displayed is also order driven. The Tokyo Stock Exchange is a pure order-driven exchange.

In addition to prices, the limit order book also records the number of shares for each order. Each price increment in the limit order book is called a step. The aggregate number of shares available at each step is called the **depth**. The depth is typically highest at the BBO and declines as prices move away from the BBO. Some markets display the entire limit order book, some display the five best bids and asks, and some display just the BBO.

We turn to consideration of what happens when a new limit order is entered. If a trader places a limit order to buy at 20.10, which is higher than the BBO bid, but less than the BBO ask, the new BBO bid will be 20.10 and the spread will decrease. We have discovered that spreads are a source of revenue for dealers. But spreads are also costs for traders. The strategy of placing limit orders that improve the BBO might be used by a trader trying to pay a smaller spread. However, liquidity suppliers face **picking off risk**, the risk that an informed party will take advantage of a **stale price** that reflects out of date information or at a price that informed traders know does not reflect the stock's true value.

If a new limit order is placed at a price that is inferior to the BBO, which is sometimes called away from the BBO or away from the market, the limit order joins the queue at the limit order price. This limit order strategy might be used by a trader who hopes to get a bargain or who wants to participate in trades as the market moves over various prices.

If a new limit order to buy (sell) is placed at the BBO ask (bid) there are several possibilities, depending on the size (number of shares) in the order. If the size is less than the depth already in the limit order book at that price, the order will be immediately executed and the depth will fall. If the order's size exactly matches the depth currently in the limit order book, the order will be immediately executed, and the BBO will have a higher ask (lower bid), increasing the spread. If its size is more than the current depth the order will be executed for that depth, but what happens to the remaining part of the order varies from market to market. In most markets the unexecuted portion becomes part of the limit order book at the limit order price. These markets do not allow an order to **walk up (or down) the limit order book.**

Suppose that the best ask is for 1,000 shares at 3.01 and the next best ask is for 1,200 shares at 3.02. If a trader places a limit order to buy 2,200 shares at 3.02, what will happen? In some markets the trader will receive an execution for 1,000 shares at 3.01 and the remainder of the order will become a limit order to buy 1,200 shares at 3.01. If the order is allowed to walk up the book, the trader will receive an execution for 1,000 shares at 3.01 and for 1,200 shares at 3.02. One purpose of preventing orders from walking up or down the book is to prevent orders at erroneous prices from executing. Suppose that instead of entering an order to buy at 3.02 the trader entered an order to buy at 4.02 by mistake. If the size of the order was sufficient the trader could receive an execution of shares at unintended prices. To ensure that the orders are intentional, the trader might be required to place separate orders to walk up or down the book.

When traders enter market orders or marketable limit orders, depth is removed from the limit order book. The speed with which new limit orders replace this depth on the limit order book is called **resiliency**.

The aggressiveness of order placement on the limit order book differs by trader type. By aggressiveness we mean how close a new limit orders is placed to the BBO. The most aggressive orders are immediately executed. The most aggressive orders are orders that better the BBO, followed in turn by orders at the BBO, and orders away from the BBO. Proprietary traders and hedge funds place the most aggressive orders, purchasing and trading on information about the very short term state of the market. **Mutual funds** and insurance companies are less aggressive because they focus on longer term investing. Individual investors on average are the least aggressive, probably because they are less effective in monitoring their order status and are less privy to information.

Some traders place order simultaneously at multiple prices on the limit order book. This practice places their orders closer to the front of the queue at each price step, making execution more likely if prices move.[1] Placing orders simultaneously at multiple prices might also make sense as part of a strategy to achieve an execution price equal to the volume weighted trading price for the day.

A new trend in secondary markets is **high-frequency trading**. (HFT can stand for high-frequency trading or high-frequency traders, depending on the context.) HFTs employ sophisticated computer algorithms to place orders. If not executed, these orders are often cancelled within milliseconds. HFTs typically do not hold inventory positions overnight. HFTs have low **latency**, which is the speed with which they are able to communicate with the trading venue. Latency is limited by the speed of light. HFTs account for a majority of total trading volume in U.S. equities.

High-frequency traders follow a number of strategies. Tradebot uses sophisticated computers and software and colocation to achieve extremely low latency.[2] Tradebot places limit orders that supply liquidity.[3] Other firms use past price relationships (called **statistical arbitrage**) between two stocks (which is **pairs trading**) to determine when one is overvalued relative to the other.

Some argue that high-frequency trading has destabilized markets. On the afternoon of May 6th, 2010, at about 2:40 pm, U.S. stocks suffered one of the most severe sell-offs in history, with the Dow Jones Industrial Average (DIJA) dropping almost 1,000 points in a matter of minutes.[4] This event is popularly called the Flash Crash. Over 20,000 trades over more than 300 stocks were executed at prices that differed 60% or more from their 2:40 pm prices. Several stocks experienced extreme prices of either 0.01 USD or 100,000 USD (see Table 2-3). Stocks recovered a significant portion of the loss later the same day. For example, ACON opened at 18.90 USD and closed at 18.86 USD, but during the period of the Flash Crash had several

---

[1] Aitken, Almeida, Harris, McInish (2009).

[2] Lucchitte, Aaron, Companies seek edge through speed as computer trading expands, 2006. Wall Street Journal, p. A12, December 15, 2006.

[3] http://tradebotsystems.com/

[4] Report (2010).

trades at 0.01 USD.[1] After the market close, the exchanges and FINRA met and agreed to cancel these trades because they were clearly erroneous. On March 22, 2012, the BATS exchange had its initial public offering after the market close. As trading began the next day a technological glitch caused the shares' price to fall to a few cents within seconds. Several other stocks were also affected. The exchange was forced to cancel its IPO.[2]

4.3. Call markets

Call markets solve the problem of matching liquidity demand and supply by concentrating trading at a single point in time. We describe the daily London gold price fixing, which is a call, in Box 2-1. Before a **call trade** orders accumulate during a non-trading period and the market opens at a specified time or under specified circumstances.[3] On some markets the timing of the call is randomized to mitigate gaming. Once the time to trade arrives, the accumulated orders are examined and buyers and sellers who are willing to trade at a given price are matched using an algorithm. The algorithm is typically complicated, but they are designed to achieve certain objectives such as maximizing the number of shares traded, or minimizing the change in price.

Many stock exchanges, including the Australian Securities Exchange (ASX), use a call to open and close trading.[4] The ASX uses the same algorithm to restart trading after a trading halt or suspension. The Taiwan Stock Exchange (TSE) operates a computer-based call market. The TSE opens a stock for trading, executes the orders that can be executed, closes trading in that stock, and then moves on to the next stock. Once all the listed stocks have been examined the process begins again with the first stock. Since the entire procedure is computerized there are only a few minutes between each call.

---

[1] McInish, Upson and Wood (2013).

[2] http://online.wsj.com/article/SB10001424052702304636404577299560502440118.html

[3] A call trade is also called a **batch trade**.

[4] The algorithm used by the Australian Stock Exchange can be found at: http://www.asx.com.au/resources/education/basics/open_Close.htm

4.4. Open outcry

Historically, most futures exchanges operated a trading floor and used a method of trading called **open outcry**. Traders stand on steps arranged so that they can see each other. Because each step is typically depressed below

Table 2-3. Firms experiencing extreme trade prices during the Flash Crash

On May 6 there are 20 stocks that trade at an extreme price, which is a price of 0.01 or 100,000 dollars. For these 20 stocks, we present the following information: Open, the first trade of the day at or after 9:30 am; Close, the last trade price at or before 4:00 pm; Extreme price, which is 1 cent or $100,000.

Symbol	Open	Close	Extreme Price
ACN	41.94	41.11	0.01
ACOM	18.90	18.86	0.01
BGS	11.00	10.07	0.01
BRO	19.69	19.01	0.01
CASY	37.76	36.62	0.01
CNP	14.39	13.84	0.01
EXC	43.35	41.92	0.01
EXP	31.48	30.71	0.01
G	16.31	15.94	0.01
ITC	53.27	51.53	0.01
IWA	16.78	16.20	0.01
LEA	77.10	73.88	0.01
RDN	10.95	9.75	0.01
SAM	59.44	56.01	0.01
VRGY	11.22	11.02	0.01
AAPL	253.83	246.05	100,000.00
AMLN	19.41	18.53	100,000.00
AMSC	27.34	25.89	100,000.00
BID	34.61	33.00	100,000.00
EQIX	94.70	92.79	100,000.00

Source: McInish, Upson, and Wood (2014).

Box 2-1. An example of a call market: The London daily gold fixing

An example of a call market is the London gold fixing that occurs twice each business day at 10:30 am and 3 pm London time. All trades are consummated at a single price. The actual market is really a wholesale market and a round lot is one bar of 400 troy ounces. However, the price set in the fix is used by many traders and merchants to set their own prices.

Five banks participate in the fixing, but these banks represent many buyers and sellers. Historically the fix price was only in BGP, but now USD and EUR prices are also determined. Typically, it takes about 10 to 15 minutes to arrive at or fix the price, but the process has taken over two hours. The participating banks charge buyers a fee of 20 cent per troy ounce. However, since the five participating banks are acting as market makers, some argue that these banks make more profit by trading using their knowledge of their firm's orders than from the spread. The fix is now done by telephone.

At the beginning of the meeting the chair announces a starting price. Each of the five banks announces whether they are a buyer or seller at that price and the amount. If the amounts sought and offered do not equal, the chair announces the net balance sought or offered. The price is adjusted upward if there are more buyers than sellers and downward if there are more sellers than buyers at the state price. During the entire process the participating banks are in touch with their own dealing rooms and their clients to assess buying and selling demand. Participants can ask for a short break in the process by announcing 'flag.' This is a carryover from when the fixing was done face to face and the participants actually raised a flag to request a halt. The price adjustments continue until an equilibrium price is reached and the chair declares the price is fixed. Typically, the fix price indicates that buying and selling demand are within 25 bars of each other.

Source:
http://www.galmarley.com/framesets/fs_trading_physical_gold_faqs.htm

floor level, one below the other, the location of trading is called the **pit.** Traders shout out their orders (and also use hand signals) to indicate whether they are buyers or sellers and at what price. Other traders willing to take the opposite side of the trade shout and signal their acceptance. The trader making the original offer is typically expected to trade with the first responding trader.

5. Exchanges and alternative trading systems

As the name indicates, secondary market trades occur in markets. We consider two types: exchanges and alternative trading systems.

5.1. Exchanges

An **exchange** is an organization whose members or participants trade securities among themselves at a fixed location, which can be either a computer or a trading floor. Table 2-4 shows the 10 largest exchanges in the world in terms of value of listed equities. A list of U.S. exchanges and their web addresses is provided in Table 2-5. Nonmembers such as public investors can trade securities listed on an exchange by opening an account with a member. The member is generally required to collect information to make sure that its clients can pay for purchases or deliver assets sold. In the U.S. brokerage firms that make recommendations are required to ascertain that the recommendation is suitable given the needs and circumstances of the client. Brokerage firms call employees dealing with the public different

Table 2-4. Largest exchanges, by value of stocks listed at year end

		Value (billion USD)	
Rank	**Exchange**	**2012**	**2011**
1	NYSE Euronext (U.S.)	14,086	11,796
2	NASDAQ (U.S.)	4,582	3,845
3	Tokyo Stock Exchange Group	3,479	3,325
4	London Stock Exchange Group	3,397	3,266
5	NYSE Euronext (Europe)	2,832	2,447
6	Hong Kong Stock Exchange	2,832	2,258
7	Shanghai SE	2,547	2,357
8	TMX Group	2,059	1,912
9	Deutsche Borse	1,486	1,185
10	Australian SE	1,387	1,198

Source: World Federation of Exchanges, 2012 WFE Market Highlights.

names. Registered representatives and financial planners are just two of these. There is a growing trend for customers to place orders with their broker online without any direct assistance. Some brokers provide select clients with tools for placing orders directly on an exchange's limit order book, which is called **direct market access.**

There has been a worldwide movement to consolidate exchanges. In 2005 the Archipelago Exchange acquired the Pacific Exchange. In 2006 the New

Table 2-5. U.S. exchanges

In February 2013 there are 16 exchanges registered with the U.S. securities and Exchange Commission as national securities exchanges.

Exchange	Web address
NYSE MKT LLC	https://nyse.nyx.com/
BATS Exchange, Inc.	http://www.batstrading.com/
BATS Y-Exchange, Inc.	http://www.sec.gov/rules/sro/byx.shtml
BOX Options Exchange LLC	http://www.bostonoptions.com/
NASDAQ OMX BX, Inc.	http://www.nasdaqomx.com/
C2 Options Exchange	http://www.c2exchange.com/
Chicago Board Options Exchange, Incorporated	http://www.cbsx.com/
Chicago Stock Exchange, Inc.	http://www.chx.com/
EDGA Exchange, Inc.	https://www.directedge.com/
EDGX Exchange, Inc.	https://www.directedge.com/
International Securities Exchange, LLC	http://www.ise.com/
The Nasdaq Stock Market LLC	http://www.nasdaq.com/
National Stock Exchange, Inc.	http://www.nsx.com/
New York Stock Exchange LLC	https://nyse.nyx.com/
NYSE Arca, Inc.	http://usequities.nyx.com/markets/nyse-arca-equities/
NASDAQ OMX PHLX, Inc.	http://www.phlx.com/

Source: http://www.sec.gov/divisions/marketreg/mrexchanges.shtml

York Stock Exchange and the Archipelago Exchange merged to form the NYSE Group.[1] In 2000, Amsterdam Exchanges merged with the exchanges in Brussels and Paris to form Euronext. NYSE Group acquired Euronext in 2007.[2] In late 2012 the IntercontinentalExchange announced it had reached an agreement to acquire NYSE Euronext for 8.2 billion USD.[3] In October 2012 the Tokyo Stock Exchange and the Osaka Securities Exchange announced that they had agreed to merge.

In the U.S. exchanges report trades to the **Consolidated Trade System** and quotes to the **Consolidated Quotation System (CQS).** These two systems are administered by the **Consolidated Tape System.** Non-exchanges report their trades and volume to a **Trade Reporting Facility**. A **lit** market reports its best bids and asks to the CQS and a **dark market or pool** does not. **Electronic Communications Networks** (ECNs), which are computer systems for trading outside an exchange, can be dark or lit, depending on the information they provide to the CQS. However, only exchanges can be identified on the ticker individually. Non-exchange trading venues report to a Trade Reporting Facility (TRF). Most exchanges and ECNs operate on a **maker/taker system** in which liquidity providers receive a credit when one of their orders is executed and liquidity demanders pay a fee when one of their orders is executed. **Transparency** is the information available to the market with more transparent markets providing more information. Pre-trade transparency is the information available prior to a trade and post-trade transparency is the information available after a trade. Even dark venues provide information to the market through the TRF.

Typically, only listed securities are traded on an exchange, although some exchanges allow trading in certain unlisted securities. **Listed** means that a security meets the exchange's requirements and has been approved for trading. Firms have to pay fees to have their shares traded on most exchanges. Trading that takes place off an exchange is called **over-the-counter**. Most fixed-income securities and foreign exchange trades are over

---

1 http://www.nyse.com/pdfs/nysegrouptimeline.pdf

2 http://www.nyx.com/who-we-are

3 http://www.nbcnews.com/business/nyse-multibillion-dollar-buyout-deal-ice-1C766276

the country. Equities and derivatives have large markets both on exchanges and over-the counter.

Most exchanges operate a **continuous market** that permits counterparties to trade with each other whenever they can agree on a price. Many exchanges open and close trading with a call market. Exchanges often specialize in a particular product types such as equities, fixed income securities, derivatives or foreign exchange. The World Federation of Exchanges is a trade group of 52 stock, futures, and options exchanges.[1]

The same asset is often traded on multiple exchanges. Many firms are simultaneously listed on exchanges in the U.K., U.S. and Japan for example. Even within the U.S. a given stock may trade on many exchanges. Each exchange maintains its own limit order book. Time priority is not honored across exchanges. However, the Consolidated Tape disseminates the official **National Best Bid Offer (NBBO)**. The **Order Protection Rule** (Securities and Exchange Commission Rule 611) requires that orders be executed at the NBBO or better. If an exchange receives an order and is not able to give NBBO execution, the order must be sent to another exchange that is posting the NBBO unless an exception applies. If an exchange executes a trade at a price inferior to the NBBO, the exchange has committed a trade through, and can be fined unless an exception to the Order Protection Rule applies.

Modern exchanges are very concerned with the speed at which orders are executed, which is governed by the venue's latency. For example, in 2010 the BATS Exchange acknowledged or executed trades in less than 250 microseconds on average. Even though orders travel over fiber optic cables at the speed of light, many traders have found that their orders are disadvantaged if they are located at a distance from the exchange. Hence, there is a trend for traders to demand to be able to **co-locate** their own computers next to the exchange computers. The demand for co-location is driven by **algorithmic trading**, trading where decisions are made by a computer. Because there is no human involvement in the trading decision, trades can be executed extremely quickly.

Because of the drastic reduction in latency over the last several decades, quotes can change on an exchange faster than they can be disseminated and

---

[1] http://www.world-exchanges.org/about-wfe

received by other exchanges. Exchanges do not know the instantaneous quotations of the other exchanges. Consequently, the U.S. Securities and Exchange Commission adopted the **Benchmark Exception** to the Order Protection Rule, which permits trades at prices inferior to the NBBO as long as they are at Benchmark Prices. A **Benchmark Price** is a price equal to the least aggressive (i.e., the worst) bid and ask quote over the last 1 second.[1]

Some institutional traders objected to strict enforcement of the Order Protection Rule because in theory an order could be rerouted from exchange to exchange in a never-ending cycle, never receiving an execution. These institutions argued that in some case certainty of execution is more important than receiving the best price. As a result, the U.S. Securities and Exchange Commission created an Intermarket Sweep Order (ISO) as an exception to the Order Protection Rule. An ISO is not rerouted and is executed on the exchange to which it is sent. However, the originator of an ISO is also required to submit ISOs to all other markets quoting the NBBO with sufficient size to take out all top of the book quotes.

In March 2010 the Tokyo Stock Exchange introduced a trading platform called Arrowhead that reduced execution times from several seconds to several milliseconds. As a result high-frequency trading increased from 0 to more than 30% of trading volume. Also, alternative trading venues have begun to capture a share of the Japanese market.

Historically, exchanges were mutual organizations owned by their members. There has been a rush to demutualize exchanges and convert them to regular public companies. Equity exchanges often list their own shares on their own exchange and futures exchanges list their shares on equity exchanges.

5.2. Alternative trading systems

Alternative Trading Systems (ATSs) bring buyers and sellers together electronically via call markets, crossing networks, and Electronic

---

[1] The U.S. SEC uses the term Flicker Price. However, to avoid confusion with another use of that term, McInish and Upson (2013) created the terms benchmark exception and benchmark price.

Communications Networks (ECNs). In the European Union MiFID allowed the establishment of ECN equivalents called Multilateral Trading Facilities (or MTFs).[1] ECNs are computer-based systems for trading securities that operate as virtual exchanges.[2] ATSs allow buy-side traders to avoid showing their orders to a broker. **Buy-side** refers to institutional investors such as pension funds, mutual funds, and hedge funds and to individuals. The **sell-side** are brokers and investment bankers. Unlike traditional brokers, many ATSs do not engage in proprietary trading. Hence, ATSs eliminate or minimize broker-customer agency problems.

5.2.1. Electronic communications *networks*

In 1998 the U.S. Securities and Exchange Commission authorized the creation of ECNs. As mentioned above, MTFs in the European Union are the equivalent of ECNs.[3] A list of ECNs and their web addresses is provided in Table 2-6. Hereafter, for simplicity, we will only refer to ECNs.

There was a spate of ECN formation in the years immediately after they were authorized. In 2000 ECNs accounted for 30% of NASDAQ volume, but most of the original ECNs were either acquired by exchanges or became exchanges.[4] As of September 2011, the European Securities and Markets Authority identified more than 140 MTFs operating in continental

---

[1] ECNs were authorized in the U.S. in 2006 as part of the Regulation National Market System. MTFs were authorized in the EU in 2007 as part of the Markets in Financial Instruments Directive. In 2010, 65% or European volume was on the primary markets and 35% on MTFs. Of the 35%, 16 percentage points was dark (see Brandes and Domowitz, 2010).

[2] Virtual exchange means: being an exchange practically, although not in actually.

[3] http://www.youtube.com/watch?v=Vzly3-0Luc8

[4] The London Stock Exchange and 12 brokerage firms own Turquoise, which offers trading in about 2,000 Europe securities and US-listed securities. It claims a market share in pan-European stocks of between 4 and 5 percent. http://www.ft.com/cms/s/0/8ae51556-a33b-11df-8cf4-00144feabdc0,stream=FTSynd,s01=1.html

Europe and the UK.[1] In a study using data from 2010, European dark pools were found to have trading costs 13% lower than those of the regulated primary markets.[2]

ECNs operate like exchanges, often having a limit order book, but deal with institutional clients. The order books are fully functional collecting the orders of liquidity suppliers and against which liquidity demanders can execute. ECNs allow buy-side traders to deal with each other anonymously without going through a broker. Anonymity on ECNs minimizes **frontrunning** and aids buy-side traders to keep their strategies secret.

Table 2-6. Selected ECNs

ECN/Web address	Type of security traded
Baxter-FX	forex
baxter-fx.com	
Hotspot FX	forex
hotspotfx.com/overview/index.jsp	
Fastmatch	forex
http://www.fastmatchfx.com/	
Track ECN	equities
trackecn.com	
Brut ECN	equities
rfpconnect.com/organization/the-brass-utility-llc-br	
Chi-X Japan	equities
http://www.chi-x.jp/about-us.html	

Source: Prepared by authors.

5.2.2. Dark Pools

5.2.2.1. Crossing networks

Crossing networks collect orders and periodically at more or less fixed times examine the orders to determine if there are buys and sells for the same stock. If so the stocks are crossed at the mid-point of the BBO. The

[1] http://mifiddatabase.esma.europa.eu/ and http://www.marketswiki.com/mwiki/Multilateral_Trading_Facility

[2] Brandes, and Domowitz, (2011).

exact time of the match typically varies over 1-2 minutes to avoid gaming. Alternately, the network can accumulate orders that are executed when there are matches. Instinet operates several types of crosses in Japan.[1] Other firms operating crossing networks include: Pipeline,[2] SIGMA X,[3] Liquidnet,[4] and Posit Crossing.[5]

5.2.2.2. Internalization

Some brokers, called internalizers, operate platforms that allow them to trade as the counterparty with their customers. These trades typically offer a small amount of price improvement, sometimes as little as 0.0001 USD per share. The dark pools operated by internalizers are profit centers for the broker. Fidelity CrossStream provides advanced order types such as mid-point orders.[6]

5.2.2.3. Exchange- and consortium-based hidden pools

Consortium-based dark pools are operated by groups of brokers. In February 2013 LEVEL indicated that its average daily volume was about 47 million shares and that its client received average price improvement of 0.006598 per share.[7]

5.2.2.4. Ping destinations

Ping destinations set up by hedge funds or electronic market makers allow institutional customers to submit immediate or cancel orders. The ping destination operator decides immediately whether to accept all or part of the order. The operator is the counterparty to the customers' orders. ATD has been a pioneer in this type of trading venue.[8]

---

[1] http://instinet.com/includes/pdf/asia/JapanCrossing_.pdf

[2] http://www.pipelinefinancial.com/

[3] http://gset.gs.com/offering/execution.asp

[4] http://www.liquidnet.com/products/supernatural.html

[5] http://www.itg.com/offerings/posit-crossing/posit-marketplace/

[6] https://fiiscontent.fidelity.com/RD_13569_19501/index.htm

[7] http://www.levelats.com/

[8] http://www.atdesk.com/index.html

6. Summary

Secondary markets are markets for trading securities among investors. This chapter covers four main topics related to secondary markets. First, we describe the benefits of secondary markets—liquidity and price discovery. Liquidity is the ability to sell an asset readily at a fair price. Liquid assets are worth substantially more that less liquid assets, reducing the cost of capital. Price discovery is the process of finding the equilibrium value of an asset. Knowledge of this value aids in determining the best uses of capital.

Second, we cover mechanics associated with trading. We describe the most commonly used order types—market orders, limit orders, and stop orders—and more sophisticated order types. We consider the minimum permitted price changes and how that determines the spread, the difference between the best offer price to sell (the bid) and the best offer price to buy (the ask). We describe the usual units of trading called round lots, and what determines the chronology in which orders are executed.

Third, we present four ways of trading. The principal question is who supplies liquidity by being willing to be a counterparty to traders who wish to trade immediately. In some markets dealers continually stand ready to buy from or sell to investors. In other markets, limit orders that cannot be immediately executed because there are no counterparties willing to trade at the set price are available for other traders to trade against. Call markets concentrate trading at points in time so buyers and sellers can meet. Orders are accumulated during non-trading periods. The market is opened and orders whose counterparties can agree on a price are executed. Then the market is closed. In the fourth method, traders stand in a crowd and shout out their orders to buy and sell, trading with counterparties who accept the offers.

Fourth, we describe exchanges where members trade with each other. Trading also occurs off exchanges in Alternative Trading Systems, including crossing networks and Electronic Communication Networks (ECNs). Crossing networks allow buy-side traders to match orders to buy and sells among themselves at particular times of the trading day. ECNs allow buy-side traders to trade vis-à-vis a limit order book that is not a part of an exchange.

Questions

1. Why is liquidity important?
2. Contrast price discovery in primary and secondary markets.
3. Explain three motivations that a trader might have for placing a limit order.
4. Describe at least one pro and one con for using a market order.
5. Identify the three components of the spread and why each exists.
6. Comparing call markets and continuous markets identify one advantage that each has over the other.
7. What advantages do buy-side traders achieve by using ECNs?
8. Why might a trader achieve lower transactions costs by using a crossing network rather than an exchange?

References

Amihud, Yakov and Haim Mendelson. 1988, Liquidity, volatility, and exchange automation, Journal of Accounting, Auditing and Finance 3, 369-395.

Aggarwal, Reena, 2000, Stabilization activities by underwriters after initial public offerings, Journal of Finance 55, 1075-1103.

Brandes, Yossi, and Ian Domowitz, 2011, Alternative trading systems in Europe, Journal of Trading 6(2), 14-21.

Crabbe, Leland E. and Christopher M. Turner, 1995, Does the liquidity of a debt issue increase with its size? Evidence from the corporate bond and medium-term note market, Journal of Finance 50, 1719-1734.

Ding, David K., Frederick H. deB. Harris, Sie Ting Lau, and Thomas H. McInish, 1999, An investigation of trading in Malaysia and Singapore: price discovery in informationally-linked markets, Journal of Multinational Financial Management 9, 317-329.

Domowitz, Ian, 1996, An exchange is a many-splendored thing: the classification and regulation of automated trading systems, in The Industrial Organization and Regulation of the Securities Industry, Andrew Lo, ed., National Bureau of Economic Research Conference Report. Chicago: The University of Chicago Press.

Goldberg, Stuart C., 1979, Securities law (part I): recognizing fraudulent broker-dealer practices, Trial, 42-68.

Gomber, Peter, Ende Bartholomaus, and Markus Gsell, 2009, Order handling of institutional investors, Journal of Trading 4(4), 10-31.

Harris, Lawrence E., 1990, Liquidity, Trading Rules, and Electronic Trading Systems. Monograph 1990-4. New York: New York University Salomon Center.

Karolyi, Andrew, 1998, Why do companies list shares abroad? A survey of the evidence and its managerial implications, Financial Markets, Institutions and Instruments 7, 1-60.

Kissell, Robert, and Hans Lie, 2011, U.S. exchange auction trends: Recent opening and closing auction behavior, and the implications of order management strategies, Journal of Trading 6(1), 10-30.

Holthausen, Robert W., Richard W. Leftwich, and David Mayers, 1987, The effect of large block transactions on security prices, Journal of Financial Economics 19, 237-267.

International Organization of Securities Commissions. 1992, Transparency on Secondary Markets. Milano: International Organization of Securities Commissions, December.

Jayaraman, N., Kuldeep Shastri, and K. Tandon, 1993, The impact of international cross listings on risk and return: the evidence from American Depository Receipts, Journal of Banking and Finance 17, 91-103.

Lau, Sie Ting, J. David Diltz, and Vincent P. Apilado, 1994, Valuation effects of international stock exchange listings, Journal of Banking and Finance 18, 743-755.

Longstaff, Francis A., 1995, How much can marketability affect security values?, Journal of Finance 50, 1767-1774.

McInish, Thomas H. and Robert A. Wood, 1986, Adjusting for beta bias: an assessment of alternate techniques, Journal of Finance 41, 277-286.

McInish, Thomas, James Upson, and Robert Wood. 2014, The Flash Crash: Trading aggressiveness, liquidity supply and the impact of intermarket sweep orders, Financial Review 49, 481-509.

Miller, Darius P., 1999, The market reaction to international cross-listings: evidence from depositary receipts, Journal of Financial Economics 51, 103-123.

New York Stock Exchange, 1990, NYSE--Financial Executives Institute Study on Market Volatility and Investor Confidence, in Market Volatility and Investor Confidence. New York: New York Stock Exchange.

O'Hara, Maureen, 2010, What is a quote?, Journal of Trading 5(2), 10-16.

Pratt, Shannon, 1981, Valuing a business. Homewood, IL: Dow Jones-Irwin.

Report of the staffs of the CFTC and SEC to the Joint Advisory Committee on Emerging Regulatory Issues, 2010. Findings Regarding the Market Events of May 6, 2010. September 30. Downloaded from http://www.cftc.gov/ucm/groups/public/@otherif/documents/ifdocs/staff-findings050610.pdf.

Schwert, G. William, 1990, Stock market volatility, Financial Analysts Journal 46, 23-34.

Silber, William L., 1991, Discounts on restricted stock: The impact of illiquidity on stock prices, Financial Analysts Journal 47, 60-64.

Sparrow, Chris, and Denis Ilijanic, 2010, The value of liquidity, Journal of Trading 5(1), 10-15.

Stoll, Hans R., 1993, Equity trading costs in-the-large, Journal of Portfolio Management 19, 41-50.

Wall Street and Technology Magazine--recommended for insights on how technology affects financial markets.

CHAPTER THREE

TRANSACTIONS COSTS

Key Terms

Adverse information costs—the costs incurred or anticipated by a dealer as a result of trading with counterparties who have superior insight into the appropriate equilibrium price of the asset.

Agent—a broker/dealers who is buys or sells an asset as a customer's representative.

Best execution—the requirement that a broker execute a trade in such a way that the client receives the best terms.

Bid-ask bounce—a trade at the bid followed by a trade at the ask or a trade at the ask followed by a trade at the bid.

Commission—a direct charge that broker/dealers make for executing orders when acting as agents.

Directed—a client or investment manager designates that the order be given to a specific brokerage firm for execution.

Direct transaction costs—same as explicit transactions costs.

Dealer spread—the quoted spread of a particular dealer.

Effective half-spread— the trade price minus the quote midpoint divided by 2.

Execution costs-see implicit transactions costs.

Explicit transactions costs—costs of trading that typically can be identified and paid for directly such as commissions, taxes, and information costs.

Gaming—taking advantage of knowledge about events that have already occurred to enhance one's performance against a benchmark.

Implicit transaction costs—costs of executing a transactions that are not itemized and paid for directly such as the bid-ask spread, market-impact costs, and opportunity costs.

Implementation shortfall—A method of assessing the impact of transaction costs on a portfolio defined as the dollar difference or return difference between a theoretical paper portfolio with zero transaction costs and the actual portfolio of securities that are purchased or sold.

Indirect transaction costs—same as implicit transaction costs.

Information costs—The costs associated with acquiring the needed information on markets or securities required to trade.

Inventory holding costs—the costs incurred or anticipated by a dealer as a result of inventory positions acquired in the process of market making.

Market impact—the change in market price resulting from the execution of an order.

Price impact—see market impact.

Price improvement—trading at a price between the best bid and ask.

Market spread—the difference between the best ask and the best bid quoted in the market.

Markup/markdown—a direct charge that broker/dealers make for executing orders as principal.

Opportunity costs—the lost profit from trades that are missed or not executed due to changes in market conditions before the order can be completed.

Order processing costs—the costs associated with supplying liquidity such as the cost of equipment and employees.

Principal—a broker/dealers who is a party to the transaction with the client rather than an agent.

Quoted half-spread—one-half of the ask minus the bid.

Soft dollars—in the U.S., a rebate provided by brokerage firms to investment managers for use in purchasing anything that materially aids in investment management.

Spread—the difference between the ask and bid.

Transaction costs—all of the costs associated with a transaction including the costs of failing to execute the trade.

Tick size—the minimum allowable price variation..

Trader—an employee of a firm who has the responsibility of executing buy and sell orders.

Volume Weighted Average Price (VWAP)—The average transaction price of a security weighted by trade volume.

IN THIS CHAPTER, we discuss two main topics

- The importance and characteristics of transactions costs, and
- Types of transaction costs such as commissions, the bid-ask spread, and information costs.

Then, we deal with the measurement of transactions costs.

1. Introduction

Increasingly, investors realize that the cost of buying and selling their investments is an important determinant of the return these investments achieve. In the first part of this chapter, we describe explicit and implicit transaction costs. Explicit transactions costs include commissions and information costs. Implicit transactions costs, also called execution costs, include several costs such as the difference between the price at the time the decision to buy or sell is made and the price actually paid, and the bid-ask spread. The second part of this chapter deals in greater detail with the measurement quantification of transactions costs, especially the difficulties in quantifying implicit transactions costs. We present the results of previous studies that attempt to quantify the level of transactions costs for equity portfolios.

Implicit trading costs can be more than three times as high as explicit transactions costs. Traders of all sizes should pay careful attention to the transaction costs of trading investments in order to maximize their return on investment.

2. Types of transactions costs

Broadly defined, **transactions costs** are all of the costs associated with the management of investments, including the time involved in making investment decisions.[1] Transactions cost can be classified as direct or indirect, or, alternately, as explicit or implicit. **Direct or explicit transactions costs** are itemized separately and investors pay for these just like any other expenses. The most common explicit transactions costs are the fees charged by an investment banker or broker for buying or selling as asset for a customer. If the investment banker is a party to the transaction, the investment banker is acting as a **principal** and charges a fee called a **markup/markdown**. If the investment banker is simply the representative of the customer, the investment banker is acting as an **agent** and charges a fee called a **commission.** Recall that markdown is the difference between the amount a dealer receives for an asset and the amount the customer receives while a markup is the difference between the amount a dealer pays for an asset and the amount the dealer receives from a customer. Other explicit transactions costs include the costs of acquiring information, taxes and transfer fees. Explicit transactions costs are administratively set or negotiated. **Information costs** are the costs required to obtain the necessary information needed to trade.

We also consider four **implicit transactions costs** or **execution costs**. The bid-ask **spread** is the cost involved in providing immediacy. **Price impact** or **market impact** is the cost resulting from any change in market price due to the execution of an order. **Market-timing costs** are incurred when the stock's price moves in response to factors unrelated to the particular transaction before the transaction can be executed. Rushing a trade to reduce market-timing costs may result in higher market impact costs. Market-timing costs are a cost of executing a trade. A trader who fails to execute a desired trade may incur **opportunity costs**, which is the loss in profits from trades that are missed or not executed due to changes in

[1] For additional information see Schwartz and Whitcomb (1988).

market conditions before the execution can be completed. Sometimes if the market moves before an order can be completed, the remainder of the order must be abandoned.

2.1. Direct transaction costs

Direct transaction costs are less than implicit transactions costs for large traders, but nevertheless account for an important part of the cost of trading. Aitken and Swan (1997) analyze the effect of a reduction in taxes on securities transactions from 0.3% to 0.15%. These authors report an increase in share prices of 1.73%, reflecting the imputed present value of tax savings. Average volume rose 21%, which resulted in a reduction of 18% in bid-ask spreads.

2.1.1. Commissions

Commissions can vary significantly depending on the financial instrument that is being traded and the type of brokerage firm that is being used to transact the trade. Deep discount brokers, such as E*Trade®, ScotTrade®, and CharlesSchwab®, offer electronic trading at commission prices as low as 7.00 USD per stock trade in 2010.[1] Stock option commissions of roughly 9.00 USD per trade plus 0.75 USD per contract, futures commissions of 2.00 USD per trade, U.S. government bond commissions of 0 USD, and corporate bond commissions of 1 USD per bond with a minimum charge of 10 USD are examples of how commissions change depending on the type of instrument being traded for online deep discount brokers. However, if a trader asks for a broker assisted trade from an online firm, commissions quickly increase by an additional 25.00 USD to 45.00 USD per trade.

An alternative to the online broker is a full service brokerage house. Examples are Merrill Lynch®, Morgan Stanley®, and A.G. Edwards®. Full

---

[1] For example, see: TD Ameritrade, http://www.tdameritrade.com;
Bull and Bear Securities: http://www.bullbear.com/;
Charles Schwab, http://www.schwab.com/;
Fidelity Brokerage Services, http://www.fidelity.com ;
ScotTrade http://www.scottrade.com/;
E*trade https://us.etrade.com/e/t/home

service brokers differ from online firms in that the broker will offer trading advice. For example, the broker will offer research and recommendations on which stocks to purchase, ways to protect investments, the type of financial assets that should be included in an investment portfolio, and when a given investment should be sold. For this additional service, commission costs are much higher per trade, on the order of 100.00 USD per trade compared to 7.00 USD for some online firms. However, full service brokers help mitigate another explicit cost of trading, information costs. Because of the competition from online brokerage firms, full service brokers also offer online trading at significantly reduced fees compared to the full service commission.

On most exchanges worldwide, including in the U.S., commissions are negotiable, especially for large customers. It may pay for small investors to compare rates for different brokers and different types of transactions. For selected examples of commissions around the world see Table 3-1. When the USSEC forced the brokerage industry to move to negotiated rather than fixed commissions, many expected that this would lead to reduced profits in the brokerage industry. Instead, securities trading increased and the brokerage community has prospered.

Table 3-1. Commission structure on selected exchanges

Exchange	Commission Structure
New Zealand	Negotiable
Oslo	0.3-0.5% or less; negotiable
Paris	negotiable
Mumbai	2-2.5%, Max Rs 25 per contract
Montreal	Minimum C 50 USD - 75 USD
Korea	0.6% maximum; negotiable

Source:
http://www.cftech.com/BrainBank/FINANCE/WorldStockExchange.html#anchor187822 (February 2013)

As a percentage of the value of the asset, commissions on options are typically higher than for other financial assets. Commissions and markups/markdowns on fixed-income securities are probably more varied than on other types of financial instruments. Commissions and markups/markdowns on actively traded securities such as U.S. Treasury bills are low, but commissions on the bonds of smaller issuers can be high. The markups/markdowns and commissions on currencies and futures are generally lower than those on other financial instruments.

Mutual funds pay brokerage firms commissions for buying and selling investments. Brokerage firms typically rebate some of these commissions to the investment manager. These rebates are called **soft dollars**. Beginning in 1986 the USSEC allowed brokerage firms to provide the investment manager with "anything that materially aids the manager in the performance of his investment duties." In the U.S. it is estimated that 25% of annual institutional brokerage commissions are directed to brokerage firms that will provide soft dollars. **Directed** means that a client or investment manager designates that an order be given to a specific brokerage firm for execution. Soft dollars are only available on agency trades.

The practice of allowing brokerage firms to provide soft dollars to management companies has been controversial because of the obvious agency problem involved. The mutual funds pay the brokerage fee, but the management firm receives the rebated services. Management companies argue that the rebate provides additional resources that are used to improve the investment process. Others think that the mutual fund is paying twice for the same service—once when the fund pays the management fee and again when it pays brokerage commissions. It seems self-evident that a brokerage firm could charge lower commissions if it did not have the expense of soft dollars.

2.1.2. Information costs

In his article on the economics of information, Stigler (1961) argued that the more one searched the less would be the returns for that search. Paroush and Peles (1978) were the first to develop a model for the optimal search process across different product types. These authors derived several interesting propositions: (1) the optimal amount of search is an increasing function of excess expected return, (2) investors should spend search dollars where they can get the greatest uncertainty reduction for the same outlay, and (3) the incidence of ownership of high information cost investments should increase with wealth. To the extent that information costs are fixed costs, the more money one has to invest the lower the cost per unit of investment. This is one reason that wealthy investors are more likely to own high information cost investments. A related proposition is that investment types with lower information costs are likely to be more widely held.

Information costs are the costs required to obtain the necessary information needed to trade. For example, the time, effort, and energy required to learn how to use the online trading tools offered by a deep discount broker such as E*Trade® is an information cost. On the other hand, full service brokers execute trades with minimal effort on the investor's part. Information costs also include the costs of learning about the financial investments that you wish to trade. Few people randomly select a stock to purchase, but may spend hours looking over the financial reports and analyst recommendations before committing to a trade. Based on future predictions of economic performance, institutional investors, such as banks, pension funds, and mutual funds make significant investments to identify which instruments should be purchased, which should be sold, and what investment strategies should be used. Information costs for these institutional investors can be quite high. For example, the average management fee for mutual funds is 1.3% of assets in 2010. For a 100 million dollar fund, this information costs is 1.3 million USD per year. The fund manager decides which investments to sell and which to purchase, one hopes after serious and exhaustive research. It is the information developed by the fund manager that they are compensated for.

Using data collected from a survey of wealthy investors, Srivastava, McInish and Price (1984) provide evidence supporting the propositions of Paroush and Peles. These authors show that higher perceived information costs are associated with excess returns and a greater range of returns. They also show that product types that require the advice of a lawyer, accountant, or financial advisor have higher perceived information costs. Commodity funds are an example of a product type with high information costs. These were held by only 5.7% of investors with a net worth of 401,000 - 500,000 USD, but by 17.2% of investors with a net worth of over 1 million USD. On the other hand, growth common stocks, a product type with low perceived information costs, were owned by 97.1% of investors with a net worth of 401,000 - 500,000 USD and by 98.5% of investors with a net worth of over 1 million USD.

The ownership of similar types of assets goes together. Investors who become knowledgeable about residential rental property are more likely to purchase commercial rental property. Investors who learn about government bonds are more likely to purchase corporate bonds. This allows investors to make better use of their investment in acquiring knowledge. Also, the professionals an investor gets to know in making investments reinforces this concentration. Once an investor uses an investment type that requires use of a lawyer, that investor is more likely to invest in other products that also require the use of a lawyer.

When an institutional investment manager makes a decision to buy or sell, the order is typically given to the firm's **trader** for execution. Also, when a brokerage firm's retail or institutional salesperson receives an order, that order is transmitted to the brokerage firm's trader (traders work at a trading desk) for execution. Hence, in this usage a trader is an employee of a firm charged with the task of executing a buy or sell order. Box 3-1 discusses attributes of a good trader. Execution costs are the costs of actually buying whose definition one uses, may not include opportunity costs because no trade is executed.

The measurement of transaction costs has relevance for portfolio managers for a variety of reasons. Transaction costs have a direct impact on portfolio performance. Also, it is usually easier to reduce costs, say, by reducing portfolio turnover, than to increase the portfolio's returns to pay for higher transactions costs. In the U.S. the Employee Retirement Income Security Act of 1974 (ERISA) stimulated an interest in monitoring and assessing the cost of asset management (Kehrer, 1991, pp. 259-271). ERISA requires that plan assets must be used for the exclusive benefit of the plan and its participants, and fiduciaries' actions must be consistent with professional money management practices. Because transactions costs can greatly affect investment performance, those administering pension assets in the U.S. have been forced to take an active interest in assessing transactions costs. Interest in measuring and assessing transaction costs has spread to other managers as well.

The relative importance of brokerage commissions and indirect costs have implications for the strategies portfolio managers use to minimize execution

Box 3-1. What makes a good trader?

The following are a question and answer from Gilbert Beebower, executive vice president of SEI corporation, a leading U.S. provider of accounting and related services to investment and pension managers.

Question: You have probably looked at more data evaluating trading prowess than anyone in the world. What, in your opinion, distinguishes a great trader from a good trader? Have you noted any common mistakes that could be avoided?

Beebower: Trading is necessarily an integral part of the investment process. The ability to demonstrate exceptional skill as a trader depends to a large extent on how much trading flexibility the demands of the portfolio manager permit. Demands for immediacy are likely to be costly, albeit less costly, for the expert trader. A "great" trader is one who makes an effort to be a part of the investment decision-making process, thus bringing his understanding of market liquidity and trading opportunities to bear before, during, and after investment decisions are made. A "good" trader only satisfies the portfolio manager after the decision has been made.

A common mistake that lesser traders often make is to second-guess the portfolio manager as to when the trade should be executed on the basis of predicting where the price will be tomorrow or days later, not on the basis of current liquidity. If a trader can predict where prices will be tomorrow or some days later, he should be in charge of the investment process.

Source: Beebower, Gilbert, 1989, Evaluating transactions cost, in The Complete Guide to Securities Transactions, Wayne H. Wagner, ed., New York: Wiley, p. 150. Copyright © 1989. Reprinted by permission of John Wiley & Sons, Inc.

costs. In evaluating the quality of execution services provided by brokerage firms, it must be kept in mind that, despite their importance, transaction costs are not the only concern of brokerage firm clients. Another and probably more important concern is **best execution**, according to the National Association of Security Dealers: "In any transaction for or with a customer or a customer of another broker-dealer, a member and persons associated with a member shall use reasonable diligence to ascertain the best market for the subject security and buy or sell in such market so that the resultant price to the customer is as favorable as possible under prevailing market conditions."[1]

But best execution does not necessarily imply best price. In deciding whether best execution has been achieved, other factors must be considered including speed and the security involved. In comparing the execution costs of one firm with another, an inferior execution is an additional cost that must be taken into account (Macey and O'Hara 1996).

Implicit transactions costs are typically difficult to measure. One firm that monitors transaction costs is Plexus Group, Inc., which analyzes transactions costs and strategies for over 125 clients, who manage over 1.5 trillion USD in assets. Clients include domestic managers, global managers, sponsors, brokers and exchanges.[2] Factors that increase transaction costs include:[3]

> "Speed: Faster trades may demand more supply than is readily available.
>
> Size: Similarly, size of trade can overwhelm the market's ability to accommodate the transaction.
>
> Momentum: It will be more expensive to buy a stock in a crowd of buyers than in a crowd of sellers.
>
> Liquidity: Thin or dull markets extract higher transaction costs than markets that are robust and vibrant."

Table 3-2 provides information concerning the relative size of transaction costs for a large sample of mutual funds.

2.1.3. Taxes

Taxes, transfer fees and the like can have a substantial impact on the cost of trading. If costs are high the amount of trading may be significantly

---

[1]http://finra.complinet.com/en/display/display.html?rbid=2403&record_id=12795&element_id=3643&highlight=best+execution#r12795

[2] The web site for Plexus group is http://www.plexusgroup.com/

[3] Wagner and Banks (1992, p. 9).

Table 3-2. Explicit and implicit transactions costs for mutual funds

For quintiles based on asset size, for a large sample of mutual funds, we present explicit (commissions) and implicit (spread and price impact) transactions costs. The columns do not add because all values are medians.

Assets (mill. USD)	3,008	4,880	7,501	12,957	44,796
	Transactions costs (% of transaction amount)				
Commissions	0.12	0.13	0.11	0.07	0.05
Spread	0.04	0.05	0.03	0.03	0.02
Price Impact	0.48	0.97	0.38	0.43	0.37
Total Trading Cost	0.71	1.15	0.55	0.56	0.41

Source: Extracted from Kopcke, Vitagliano, and Karamcheva (2009).

reduced, damaging the liquidity of the market. The harm may be mitigated if investors can direct their trades to alternate market centers.

2.1.4. Explicit transactions costs—conclusion

Many types of explicit transaction costs, such as margin interest and management fees, continue as long as an investor owns an asset. Few people or fund managers simply purchase an investment and hold it forever. A commission or markup is typically paid both when an asset is purchased and when it is sold.[1] Mutual fund management fees are assessed regularly and individuals often spend many hours tracking the performance of their investment choices. Of course, there are taxes associated with investment profits and tax write-offs associated with investment losses once an asset is sold. These costs can significantly impact the return on an investment. For example, suppose that on investment nets a 5% annual return with poor management of transaction costs and a second firm, investing in the identical assets nets 6% return with strong management of

[1] Exceptions include IPOs, secondary distributions (http://financial-dictionary.thefreedictionary.com/Secondary+Distribution), purchase of no load mutual funds and futures, where a commission is paid to initiate the transaction but not to close it.

transaction costs. The 1% difference will result in a portfolio value that is roughly 22% larger after 20 years.

2.2. Implicit transaction costs

Implicit transaction costs often amount to several times direct costs or even more. Barclay, Kandel, and Marx (1998) find that increases in bid-ask spreads resulting in higher transaction costs significantly reduce trading volume, but do not have a significant effect on prices.

2.2.1 Bid-ask spread

2.2.1.1. Introduction

The first implicit transaction cost we discuss is the bid ask spread. Figure 3-1 displays the basic concept of the bid ask spread. A key point to understand is that if you wish to sell a stock, someone else must buy it and if you wish to buy a stock, someone else must sell it. Figure 3-1 shows a stock with a current ask price of 20.08 USD. 300 shares are for sale at this price. The bid price for the stock is 20.03 USD and 1,200 shares are sought at this price. These are passive orders, supplying liquidity. The bid ask spread is the difference between the ask and bid prices or 20.08 USD - 20.03 USD = 0.05 USD, or five cents per share traded. These passive limit

Figure 3-1. Bid-ask spread

Active				**Passive**
Buy	→	**Ask** **20.08 USD** **300 shares**	←	**Sell**
Sell	→	**Bid** **20.03 USD** **1,200 shares**	←	**Buy**

orders create the quotation displayed in the market and must wait until a trader demanding liquidity enters the market for the orders to be executed Now, consider a trader who enters an order to purchase 200 shares immediately at the best price. The order will execute at a price of 20.08 USD. Just after the order executes if the traders were to sell these 200 shares the sale price would be 20.03 USD. The trader will be required to pay two commissions, one for each trade, plus lose an additional 0.05 USD per share on the round trip trade.

Spreads are implicit transactions costs rather than explicit transactions costs because they have to be measured indirectly. For example, they are not listed on the confirmation statement. Note too that the spread is a cost for the aggressive liquidity demander and a gain for the passive liquidity supplier. The trading strategy that is chosen determines the impact of the spread. The spread is a cost of immediacy and the reward for patient trading.

Bid-ask spreads are a feature of trading when dealers are providers of immediacy. All product types considered in this book—equities, fixed-income securities, derivatives, and currencies—have bid-ask spreads. Table 3-3 shows the bid and ask quotations for the currencies of 8 countries and for the Euro on November 12, 2010 along with the percentage bid-ask spread. Bessembinder (1994) provides a discussion of bid-ask spreads in currency markets. These are quotations for transaction sizes of 1 million USD or more. Even though the spreads are relatively low, one might be able to get better quotes by shopping other dealers and on occasion one might be able to trade between the quotes. Selling at a price that is higher than the best bid or buying at a price that is lower that the best ask is called **price improvement**.

A trade at the bid followed by a trade at the ask or a trade at the ask followed by a trade at the bid reflects **bid-ask bounce**.

The implicit transactions costs of bid ask spreads are present even if the holding period is extended. Suppose you purchase 200 shares at the ask price of 20.08 USD. Later in the day the quote becomes 20.13 USD ask and 20.08 USD bid. Even though the price of the stock increased by 0.05 USD an active sell order submitted to the market would execute at 20.08 USD, netting the trader a loss if there is a commission.

Table 3-3. Bids, asks, and percentage spread for eight currencies

Currency	Bid	Ask	% Spread
Euro	1.55462	1.55462	1.55462
Japanese Yen	0.8958	0.8958	0.8958
British Pound	1.0515	1.0515	1.0515
Australian Dollar	7.7539	7.7539	7.7539
Canadian Dollar	1.2733	1.2733	1.2733
Hong Kong Dollar	13.4323	13.4323	13.4323
Singapore Dollar	1.55462	1.55462	1.55462
Mexican Peso	0.8958	0.8958	0.8958

Source: Prepared by authors. Approximate rates for 1 September 2013.

The implicit transactions costs created by bid ask spreads are significant. Every day institutions receive money from investors to invest, called cash inflows. These inflows must be invested in order to meet the return obligations of the investment fund. However, in addition to inflows, there are cash outflows as investors terminate their investments and expect cash payments from the firms they invested in. A simple example is a pension fund. Some workers are paying into the pension, saving for retirement; some workers have retired and are drawing on the pension fund to receive payments. Some day's inflows are greater than outflows and the fund will purchase assets, other day's outflows will be greater than inflows and the fund must sell assets. These round trip transactions, where a security is purchased and then sold or sold and then purchased, reduce the potential returns that a fund can achieve. The cost of bid ask spreads can be mitigated by using a passive rather than an active trading strategy.[1] The need to choose between active and passive trading strategies means that investors have to deal with two other types of implicit transactions costs—opportunity costs and implementation shortfalls, which we discuss next. Box 3-2 describes a patient-trading program initiated by RJR Investment Management. This program is estimated to have saved RJR 144,000 to

[1] The pension plan can also hold cash, but holding cash generally reduces returns because other assets typically earn more than cash.

548,000 USD on a portfolio of 40 million USD by adopting a passive rather than an active trading strategy.

Box 3-2. Passive trading

In 1988, RJR established a 40 million USD investment fund to acquire a 250-stock subset of stocks from the Russell 2000 index.† The managers estimated that it would cost from 2.5% to 3.5% of asset value to acquire these shares over a five day period. In an effort to reduce transactions cost, the managers decided to try to acquire the shares passively rather than demanding liquidity.

When the market opened each day, the fund placed "good today" limit orders on shares that had been underperforming the index. At the end of trading day orders for any shares in the 250 firms that had not been purchased were submitted to an ECN. After 75% of the total shares needed had been bought, the fund adopted a more aggressive trading strategy. And at the end of two weeks the fund purchased all shares needed to complete the portfolio using market orders.

RJR calculated Perold's (1988) implementation shortfall by comparing two portfolios—an actual portfolio and a paper portfolio. For the actual portfolio it was assumed that the entire 40 million dollars was invested in the Russell 2000 index at the initiation of the program. Then, as shares were acquired, it was assumed that the funds were acquired by selling the Russell 2000 index portfolio. Hence, this portfolio's performance reflects both movements in the Russell 2000 index and the prices actually paid for the portfolio stocks. The paper portfolio's performance was based on the prices that would have been paid had the entire portfolio been purchased immediately at the initiation of the program.

The implementation shortfall showed that the actual portfolio underperformed the paper portfolio by 2.13%, which saved the fund from 36 to 137 basis points.

Based on Bodurtha, Steven G. and Thomas E. Quinn, 1989, The patient trading program: A case study in measuring and lowering portfolio trading costs, New York: Kidder Peabody and Company.

2.2.1.2. Reasons that there is a spread

One reason that the bid ask spread exists is because suppliers of immediacy must be compensated. In many markets, dealers who must cover their costs supply this immediacy. But what are these costs? The earliest investigations of spreads focused on **order processing costs**. These include the costs of the dealer's time, paper-work costs, and transfer taxes and other expenses incurred by the dealer in providing immediacy. The dealer also incurs the cost of financing any inventory.

Another cost of providing immediacy is **inventory holding costs**.[1] Dealers may suffer losses from fluctuations in the price of an asset held in inventory. While changes in asset prices may also result in gains, in general the prospect of a loss in more influential that the prospect of a gain.

Amihud and Mendelson (1986) develop a model in which they predict that "there is a clientele effect whereby investors with longer holding periods select assets with higher spreads." Atkins and Dyl (1994) test whether higher bid-ask spreads are associated with greater holding periods as proxied by the turnover ratio for a firm's stock. For NASDAQ stocks they find that a 1% difference in spread is associated with a 1.34-year difference in investors' average holding periods and the relationship is mildly nonlinear: an increase in spread from 4% to 5% leads to a 2/3-year increase in holding period. The ratio of the turnover of the most liquid stocks to the least liquid stocks has been increasing since 1964.[2]

In many cases prices are quoted for financial products on a net basis. In other words the price paid is the price indicated and there is no explicit markup/markdown. Quotes among dealers are on a net basis. But institutions and individual traders may also receive quotes on a net basis especially if the broker is not acting as an agent. Investors should not

---

[1] An example of the inventory holding cost model is provided by Ho and Stoll (1981) who propose that after a dealer purchase bid prices are lowered to discourage additional sales and ask prices are also lower to encourage purchases from the dealer. Thus, the new bid and ask must reflect prices that make the dealer indifferent between a transaction at the bid and a transaction at the ask.

[2] Ben-Rephael, Azi, Ohad Kadan, and Avi Wohl, 2010.

assume that just because a net price is quoted that the broker is not charging a markup/markdown. In fact, in some cases the markup/markdown may be substantial.

Tick size is the minimum price variation permitted in a market. The minimum tick size is set arbitrarily by the exchange or by a regulator. Currently, on U.S. exchanges, the minimum tick size for stocks is 0.01 USD if the price is more than 1 USD, while on U.S. option exchanges the minimum tick size is 0.05 USD if the cost of the option is over 0.50 USD and 0.01 USD if the cost of the option is under 0.50 USD. Many stock markets, such as Singapore and Japan, have minimum tick sizes that change with the price of the stock. Low priced stocks have small tick sizes and as the price increases, so does the minimum tick size.

2.2.1.3. Alternate ways of defining the spread

Because of the importance of spreads as a transaction cost, a number of ways of measuring spreads have been developed. A number of these focus on the half-spread. If an investor buys at the quoted ask and then sells at the quoted bid, the entire spread has been incurred as a cost. But since there are two transactions, the cost per transaction is the half-spread. Of course, the **quoted half-spread** is simply one-half of the quoted ask minus the quoted bid. The **effective half-spread** is the trade price minus the quote midpoint (the ask plus the bid) divided by 2.[1]

Hasbrouck (2009) studies the effective spread (2 X the effective half-spread) over the years 1926 -2006. This measure peaked in the years following the stock market crash in 1929. In recent years on average the measure has been below 1% for even the smallest quartile of stocks by market capitalization and substantially below 1% for the three largest quartiles.

If quotes change as a result of trades either because of the information contained in the trade or because of inventory considerations, then a distinction should be made between dealer spreads and market spreads. The dealer spread can be greater than the market spread, but the market spread

---

[1] For studies of trading costs that use the effective half-spread see Lee (1992) and Petersen and Fialkowski (1994).

cannot be greater than the dealer spread. Suppose that there are two dealers, each with a spread of USD 0.50. One might give a quote of 10.00 to 10.50 while the other could give a quote of 10.25 to 10.75. While both dealers have a spread of 0.50, from the point of view of investors, the market spread is 0.25 which is obtained by subtracting the best bid of 10.25 from the best ask of 10.50. Thus, the **dealer spread** is the quoted spread of a dealer while the **market spread** is the difference between the best ask and the best bid quoted by all dealers in the market. The effective spread is calculated from actual trades. Hence, it reflects the quoted market spread, market impact and any undisplayed limit orders.

2.2.2. Price impact costs

The execution of an order has the potential to move the market price. Here we are talking about more than bid-ask bounce. Price impact involves moving the bid or ask either temporarily or permanently. To examine where price impact comes from we first start with a static, snap shot, example. Figure 3-2 shows a snap shot of a hypothetical limit order book. The limit order book represents all passive orders that have been submitted to the market and that are waiting for active orders to arrive to complete trades. The best bid or ask price available in the market is called the top of the book and sets the quote for the market center. The best bid price shown in Figure 3-2 is 20.03 USD, and 1,200 shares are available to trade at this price. Recall that active orders sell at the bid, but passive orders buy at the bid. As you move down the ask side of the book toward the best ask, prices decrease. The best ask price is 20.08 USD with a depth of 300 shares. Active orders buy at the ask, but passive orders sell at the ask. For example, the next best price in the ask book is 20.09 USD with a depth of 500 shares.

A naïve trader, who wishes to buy 6,000 shares of this stock might simple submit a market order. When this order executes against the ask book, 300 shares will trade at 20.08 USD, 500 shares will trade at 20.09 USD, 1,500 shares will trade at 20.11 USD, and the balance of the order, 3,700 shares, will trade at 20.15 USD. As the order executes, the price of the stock increases, which is the price impact of the trade. Although this example is easy to understand, it is based on a static, unchanging limit order book. In practice, markets are dynamic. Both active and passive orders flow into the market on a continuous basis. If the inflow of active orders, matches the inflow of passive orders, then supply meets demand, and the price of the stock typically stays constant.

Figure 3.2. Example limit order book

Bid side		Ask side	
Price	**Depth**	**Price**	**Depth**
		20.27	1,100
		20.15	4,500
		20.11	1,500
		20.09	500
		20.08	300
20.03	1,200		
20.02	1,400		
20.01	700		
19.95	5,100		
19.94	6,100		

Prepared by authors.

Before we discuss the dynamic view of price impact we need to add some additional context to the trading environment. Remember that the issue of price impact of trading is mainly the focus of large institutional traders. Large institutional investors are typically better informed about the future price changes of the market in general and of individual stocks for several reasons. First, they have a large amount of money to spend on researching the fundamental value of stocks and other financial assets. Second, the fund manager's compensation often is impacted by the fund's return performance. This means that fund managers have a strong incentive to spend research dollars wisely to find the assets likely to have the best future performance. Third, if a fund manager chooses to sell an asset, they are likely to select the asset that has the lowest potential for future performance first. How does this affect the price impact of trading?

Suppose you are able to learn that a fund will start to purchase a stock. There are two things that you can infer from this information. One is that the fund manager believes that the stock is underpriced and is expected to produce a positive return in the future. Why else would a fund manager purchase the stock? In addition, because institutional traders purchase and sell large quantities of stock, when institutions trade the added demand for liquidity will likely drive the stock price up or down in the short term. If institutions are not able to keep their trading decisions secret others can trade along with or ahead of the institutions, which will drive up their transactions costs. Traders offering liquidity in the limit order book might cancel their orders.

3. Quantifying execution costs

Explicit transaction costs can be observed and can usually be measured easily. Execution costs (implicit transactions costs), the difference between the transaction price and the "true" price of the security in the absence of a trade, are not easily measured. Although the execution price is known, the prevailing price in the absence of a trade is not observable, and therein rests the difficulty in measuring indirect execution costs. The practical alternative is to use some benchmark price as a proxy for the true price. Benchmarks can be based on pre-trade, post-trade, or average prices.[1]

3.1. Issues in quantifying execution costs

One issue that must be dealt with, whether using pre-trade or post trade performance measures, is **gaming**, the execution of a trade using knowledge of events that have already occurred to enhance the evaluation of one's performance against a benchmark. Pre-trade measures, which use prices occurring at the time of the decision to trade rather than at the actual time of the trade, are the closest approximation to a true execution cost measure. A problem with pre-trade measures is that they are subject to gaming because the trader knows the benchmark before executing the trade. If the current market price is better than the benchmark, the trader can execute the trade quickly and show favorable performance. If the comparison with the benchmark is unfavorable, the trader can delay execution or perhaps even choose not to execute the trade.

---

[1] For a discussion of these issues see Collins and Fabozzi 1991.

While it is easy to see how a pre-trade measure can be gamed, it is not as easy to recognize potential types of gaming that can occur with post-trade measures. Post-trade measures use prices occurring after the execution of the trade. Post-trade measures avoid most gaming problems, although sometimes they can be gamed in the sense that, say, a closing price could be manipulated up or down a tick with a very small transaction. Post-trade measures have the drawback of possibly being influenced by the trade itself. A good post-trade benchmark should be based on a trade occurring after the influence of the trade has dissipated. Unfortunately, this interval is neither fixed nor known; if it extends too far after the trade, the measure becomes contaminated by other variables influencing the market price and ceases to be a measure of indirect execution cost.

3.2. Value Weighted Average Price (VWAP)

Before we get into the details of VWAP trading and cost assessment, we will present the mathematical definition of VWAP and run through a brief example. Mathematically VWAP is defined as:

$$VWAP = \frac{\sum TrdV_i * Prc_i}{\sum TrdV_i} \tag{1}$$

where $TrdV_i$ is the volume of trade i and Prc_i is the price of the trade. As a quick example to demonstrate the differences between the price average and VWAP suppose that you purchase 1,000 shares of stock AB at 20 USD and then purchase another 100 shares at 25. The simple price average is (20+25)/2 = 22.5. The VWAP of your purchase is:

(20*1,000+25*100)(1,000+100)=20.46.

Table 3-4 shows several other VWAP calculation methods. Exclusion VWAP excluded the trades of the transactions being evaluated and is used when the order size is large compared to the typical trading volume. In some markets, the data required to calculate VWAP is not available or very expensive to acquire. In these cases a Proxy VWAP is calculated using reference prices such as the price average of the open, low, high, and closing price. Regardless of the method used, the VWAP calculation should have the same duration as the trade. If the order is large, say over 20 million shares, the trade may take several days or more to complete, and VWAP should be calculated over a similar number of days. If the order is to

Table 3-4. VWAP measures

Measure	Method	Comments
VWAP	Dollar volume traded in a security divided by the number of shares traded in the security.	Typical definition of VWAP, often computed on the day of the transaction. The appropriate duration of the VWAP calculation should match the duration of the trade. If the trade will take multiple days, a multiday VWAP is used.
Exclusion VWAP	Transactions that are part of the evaluated trade are not included in the VWAP measure	Applied on stocks with low trading volume where the evaluated trade represents a large fraction of the typical daily volume traded.
Proxy VWAP	Proxy VWAP with the open, low, high, and close prices.	In small foreign markets the required trade data may not be available or may be too expensive to acquire, forcing the use of a proxy.

Source: Prepared by authors.

purchase shares, then the goal of the trader is to have a VWAP of the trade that is equal to or less than the VWAP of the market, meaning that the trader executed the position below the value weighted average price of the market. If the order is to sell share the target VWAP of the trade is to be greater than or equal to the VWAP of the market. The VWAP benchmark encourages traders to spread trades out over a period of time such as a day so that the trades represent a constant proportion of the volume at each trade price. For example, in a typical day, trading volume is high at the beginning of the day, low in the middle of the day, and then high again at the end of the day. VWAP traders would then trade their position following this pattern.

Finally, traders can undertake VWAP trading, where the overall order is divided into a number of small trades and proportionality traded over the day. Firms can ask their own traders to handle the VWAP trade, arrange for a broker to execute the trade, or contract with an automated service that will execute the trade as intelligently as possible, attempting to fill the order while minimizing the price impact of the trades. This approach allows the trader to cancel the order during the trading day.

VWAP has a number of advantages and disadvantages. One of the primary advantages is that it is simple to calculate and intuitive to apply. One of the major disadvantages is that VWAP focuses only on matching the price average. To illustrate this disadvantage consider a trading day where the stock price starts at 20 USD in the morning and then finishes at 30 USD at the end of the day. VWAP traders will ignore this price trend and only trade proportional to the average volume expected in any one period.

While VWAP is still widely used as a metric and trading strategy, the Implementation Shortfall method discussed in the next section is gaining in popularity.

3.3. Implementation shortfall

One of the broadest ways of measuring transactions costs is the approach of Perold (1988). The method involves comparing the performance of two portfolios. The first is a "paper" portfolio that assumes that decisions to invest are implemented immediately at the average of the bid and ask price. The second is the performance of the portfolio actually purchased. The difference between the performances of the two portfolios is the **implementation shortfall (IS)**. If direct costs such as commissions are included, then the difference in performance is a measure of all transactions costs. If some investments are not actually made because the market moves away before the decision to invest can be implemented, then comparison of these two portfolios reveals the opportunity cost. The method also captures all the other types of execution costs. A difficulty is that the IS method requires the continuous "management" of the paper portfolio, regardless of how much it diverges from the actual portfolio. The paper portfolio must also be managed in conformance with any restrictions that limit the portfolio's investments.

As an example, at the time a trader decides to purchase a given share of stock the market price was 10 USD per share, but when the shares are actually purchased the cost is 10.50 USD. The implementation shortfall is 0.50 USD.

To illustrate the IS method consider the following case. A mutual fund manager decides to purchase X dollars of stock BC that is currently trading a price P_c, where P_c is the price at the time the decision to purchase the stock was made. If the transaction could be immediately executed without transaction costs then the fund would receive S_{BC} shares of stocks equal to X/P_c. This represents the paper value of the portfolio. The objective, from an implementation standpoint, is to come as close to the paper value as possible. In practice, the value P_c is typically fixed when the order to purchase shares is received at the trading desk that will execute the order. Assume that S_{BC} shares are actually purchased over some period of trading. At the completion of the order the value of the portfolio will be $S_{BC}*P_f$, where P_f is the market price of BC when the order is completely filled. The return on the purchased portfolio will be the ending value minus the beginning value or:

$$\text{PortfolioReturn} = S_{BC}P_f - \sum s_k p_k - \text{fixedcost} \qquad (2)$$

where s_k and p_k represent the number of shares and price of each individual trade required to execute the full order and fixed costs represent fixed costs of trading such as commissions. The return on the paper portfolio is defined as:

$$\text{Paper Return} = S_{BC}P_f - S_{BC}P_c \tag{3}$$

That is:

$$IS = (S_{BC}P_f - S_{BC}P_c) - (S_{BC}P_f - \sum s_k p_k) - \text{fixedcost}$$
(4)

or

$$IS = \sum s_k p_k - S_{BC}P_c - \text{fixedcost} \tag{5}$$

Rather than simply take the average price in the market, as VWAP attempts, traders following the IS approach are measured against the standard of perfection based on the price of the stock when the choice to purchase or sell the security was made. If the goal is to purchase shares and the stock price is trending up, the IS approach will tend to make traders more aggressive to capture shares before prices more further away from the decision price, but if prices are trending lower, they may become less aggressive, letting prices fall to reduce the implementation costs.[1]

4. Summary

In this chapter, we describe two types of transaction costs—explicit transactions costs and implicit transactions costs. Explicit transactions costs include commissions, taxes, and the like, and information costs, the costs associated with acquiring information for use in making the investment decision. In some market centers commission rates are fixed, but in others commissions are negotiable. In the U.S. many brokerage firms give investment managers credits or rebates, called "soft dollars," that can be used to purchase any items useful in managing investments.

Implicit transaction costs include market-timing costs, the loss due to a change in price as a result of factors other than a particular order, and opportunity costs resulting from losses due to failure to execute a transaction. Implicit transactions costs also include price impact costs,

---

[1] Additional information on implementation shortfall and transaction costs can be found in Kissell (2006).

which arise when executing an order causes an unfavorable change in the price of a financial instrument. Another type of implicit cost is the bid-ask spread. The bid-ask spread compensates providers of immediacy.

Sometimes exchange rules can make spreads artificially high. A tick is the minimum monetary value allowed in quoting and trading financial assets. The minimum tick size determines the minimum spread. If the minimum spread is larger than justified based on the underlying economic considerations, then spreads are artificially wide.

One way of identifying execution costs is the implementation shortfall approach in which an imaginary portfolio is acquired at the midpoint of the bid and ask at the time the decision to trade is made. The results of this imaginary portfolio are then compared with those of the actual portfolio. Another method for assessing the quality of trading is by targeting the average trading price of an order to meet or beat the Volume Weighted Average Price or VWAP.

The key point raised in this chapter is that transaction costs play an important role in determining the final return on a portfolio. Large institutional investors pay careful attention to the significant costs of trading, specifically the implicit transactions costs of trading, in order to maximize the return to investors. Small investors must balance the costs associated with gaining the require information needed to trade against the benefits and costs of allowing skilled professionals to assist them in the investment process.

Questions

1. Are financial instruments that have high information costs and/or high transactions costs more suitable for individuals with long or short investment horizons?
2. What are the strengths and weaknesses of the implementation shortfall approach to measuring transactions costs?
3. What are soft dollars and how can they affect who pays for certain investment management expenses?
4. Does a batch trade incur a bid-ask spread?
5. How can the minimum tick size affect the spread?

6. What does the term gaming mean and why is this concept important?
7. What are the components of the bid-ask spread?
8. What factors determine the size of the bid-ask spread?
9. Identify the various types of execution costs.
10. What is the concept of best execution?
11. Suppose that liquidity traders established their own market. What would be the implications for the market in which the remaining traders trade?
12. How could payment for order flow benefit retail customers?
13. Name at least two reasons that informed traders tend to place larger orders.
14. Name as least two ways that informed traders can attempt to hide their identities.

References

Amihud, Yakov, and Haim Mendelson, 1986, Asset pricing and the bid-ask spread, Journal of Financial Economics 17, 221-249.

Aitken, Michael J., and Peter L. Swan, 1997, The impact of a transaction tax on investors: the case of Australia's stamp duty reduction, Working paper, University of Sydney, Sydney.

Atkins, Allen B., and Dyl, Edward, 1991, Transactions costs and average holding periods for common stocks, Journal of Finance 52, 309 – 25.

Ben-Rephael, Azi, Ohad Kadan, and Avi Wohl, 2010, The diminishing liquidity premium, European Finance Association Conference, Bergen, 2009. http://papers.ssrn.com/sol3/papers.cfm?abstract_id=1099829

Brandes, Yossi, and Ian Domowitz, 2010, Alternative trading systems in Europe: Trading performance by European venues post-MiFID, Journal of Trading 5, 17-30.

Barclay, Michael J., Eugene Kandel, and Leslie M. Marx, 1998, The effects of transaction costs on stock prices and trading volume, Journal of Financial Intermediation 7, 130-150.

Bessembinder, Hendrik, 1994, Bid-ask spreads in the interbank foreign exchange markets, Journal of Financial Economics 35, 317-348.

Collins, Bruce M., and Frank J., Fabozzi, 1991, A methodology for measuring transaction costs, Financial Analysts Journal 47, 27-36.

Condon, Kathleen, 1981, Measuring equity transaction costs, Financial Analysts Journal 37, 57-60.

Copeland, Thomas E., and Daniel Galai, 1983, Information effects on the bid-ask spread, Journal of Finance 38, 1457-1469.

Glosten, Lawrence, and Paul Milgrom, 1985, Bid, ask and transaction prices in a specialist market with heterogeneously informed traders, Journal of Financial Economics 14, 71-100.

Hasbrouck, Joel, 2009, Trading costs and returns for U.S. equities: Estimating effective costs from daily data, Journal of Finance 64, 1445-1477.

Ho, Thomas, and Hans R. Stoll, 1981, Optimal dealer pricing under transactions and return uncertainty, Journal of Financial Economics 9, 47-73.

Kehrer, Daniel. The Pension Plan Investor. Chicago: Probus, 1991.

Kissell, Robert, 2006, The expanded implementation shortfall: Understanding transaction cost components, Journal of Trading 3, 6–16.

Kopcke, Richard W., Francis M. Vitagliano, and Zhenya S. Karamcheva, 2009, Fees and trading costs of equity mutual funds in 401(k) plans and potential savings from ETFs and commingled trusts, Working paper, Center for Retirement Research at Boston College Hovey House, Chestnut Hill, MA.

Lee, Charles, 1993, Market integration and price execution for NYSE-listed securities, Journal of Finance 48, 1009-1038.

Macey, Jonathan R., and Maureen O'Hara, 1996, The law and economics of best execution, Journal of Financial Intermediation 6, 188-223.

McInish, Thomas H., and Robert A. Wood, 1992, An analysis of intraday patterns in bid ask spreads for NYSE stocks, Journal of Finance 47, 753-764.

Paroush, Jacob, and Peles, Yoram C., 1978, Search for information and portfolio selection. Journal of Banking and Finance 2, 163 – 77.

Perold, Andre F., 1988, The implementation shortfall: paper vs. reality, Journal of Portfolio Management, 3, 4-9.

Schwartz, Robert, and David K. Whitcomb, 1988, Transaction costs and institutional investor trading strategies, Monograph Series in Finance and Economics 1988-2/3, New York University, Stern School of Business.

Srivastava, Rajendra K., McInish, Thomas H., and Price, Linda, L., 1984, Information costs and portfolio selection. Journal of Banking and Finance 8, 417–25.

Stigler, George J. 1961, The economics of information. Journal of Political Economy 69, 213–25.

Wagner, Wayne H., and Michael Banks, 1992, Increasing portfolio effectiveness via transaction cost management, Journal of Portfolio Management 19, 6-11

CHAPTER FOUR

CLEARING AND SETTLEMENT

Key Terms

Bearer—securities that are negotiable upon delivery and physical (or book-entry) possession are all that is required to effect ownership changes.

Bilateral netting—an agreement between two trading partners to exchange net amounts rather than gross amounts at settlement.

Cash (settlement)—a trade calling for settlement on the day of the trade.

Central depository—is an organization that accepts deposits of securities and that accounts for transfers of these securities among participants.

Clearing House Interbank Payments System (CHIPS)—is the largest bank clearinghouse and the leader in clearing USD payments.

Clearing member—a direct participant in a clearinghouse.

Clearing process—all the activities carried out from the time of a transaction until settlement.

Clearinghouse—a financial institution involved in clearing securities trades and also usually in some aspects of the settlement process.

Clearing—reaching an agreement about the responsibilities of each party to a securities transaction.

Credit risk—risk that a transaction will never settle for full value.

Cross margining—offsetting required margins by taking into account different types of assets owned or assets owned in different markets.

Dealing locations—in foreign exchange trading, the locations of the parties to a trade.

Declaration date—the day a company announces a forthcoming dividend.

Default—failure to settle a transaction due to economic reasons.

Delivery versus payment—settlement of the two legs of a trade occurs simultaneously.

Dematerialized—ownership records do not exist in physical form.

Errors risk—risk that an individual involved in the clearing process will make an error.

Ex-dividend—the day on and after which a purchaser of stock is not entitled a dividend.

Failed transaction—a trade that does not settle on its settlement date.

Fat finger trades—erroneous trades entered by brokerage firm employees.

Federal Reserve Wire Network (Fedwire)—a real time gross settlement system that allows the electronic transfer of USD funds among more than 9,000 participants.

Global custodians—financial institutions that ensure that clients' financial transactions are settled properly and registered correctly.

Good order—the presence of all the documents and signatures needed to effect a transfer of ownership.

Herstatt risk—See systemic risk.

Immobilized—evidence of ownership such as stock certificates are held by a depository and ownership is transferred by entries on the depositary's books.

Liquidity risk (settlement)—risk that a trade will settle for its full value, but after the agreed upon settlement time.

Margin—funds used to provide protection in case of a failure of a party in the settlement process.

Master agreement—an agreement between trading partners that stipulates that individual transactions between them are part of a single contractual relationship.

Multilateral netting—netting among more than two entities.

Netting-by-novation—an agreement between trading partners that substitutes one agreement for multiple agreements and provides for a single periodic payments.

Netting—the offsetting of obligations by trading partners so that net quantities rather than gross quantities are delivered at settlement.

Novation—the satisfaction and discharge of one contract by the substitution of a new contract.

Operational risk—risk that there will be a loss due to failure of the hardware, software, communications, or others physical aspects involved in clearing and settlement.

Out-of-balance—the amount of securities issues does not exactly match the amount authorized.

Payment date—the date on which a firm pays a dividend.

Principal risk—the risk of loss from making delivery at settlement, but, subsequently, not receiving delivery from a counterparty.

Real time gross settlement—settlement is not subject to any waiting period, payments are made in real time, and once processed payments are final and irrevocable.

Record date—the day on which an investor must own stock to be entitled to a dividend.

Registered—the identity of the owner is recorded on the books of the registrar.

Registrar—a firm, usually a financial institution, that maintains the ownership records of a securities issue and is responsible for checking that the number of shares received by the new owner equals the number of shares supplied by the old owner.

Regular way—the normal way of settling a trade.

Rematerialization—converting from virtual to physical records of ownership.

Replacement cost risk—risk due to a change in value of assets from the time of a trade until settlement.

Rolling settlement—all trades on a given day are settled on a designated subsequent day.

Settlement date—the date on which the purchaser owns the securities and the seller is entitled to receive the sales proceeds.

Settlement locations—in foreign exchange, the countries whose currency is being traded.

Settlement—the fulfillment of each party's obligation resulting from a trade.

Stock certificate—physical evidence of the ownership of stock.

Straight through processing—the transfer of data about a transaction from one step in the clearing and settlement process to the next electronically without the need for manual manipulation.

Street name—ownership is recorded in the name of a financial institution rather than in the name of the beneficial owner.

SWIFT—the global leader in providing telecommunications technology for automated cross-border payments.

Systemic risk—risk that the failure of one counterparty to meet its obligations when due will result in the inability of other counterparties to meet their obligations when due, resulting in a collapse of the entire financial system. Also known as Herstatt risk.

Trade comparison—the process of matching and confirming the terms of a trade, including the identity of the counterparties and the asset, the price and quantity, and whether there are special terms.

Transfer agent—a financial institution responsible for checking documents and effecting a change in ownership of securities.

Value date—a term used in foreign exchange trading as another name for the settlement date.

IN THIS CHAPTER, we

- Explain clearing and settlement, and
- Identify specific risks arising in clearing and settlement.

Next, three methods used to mitigate these risks are discussed, namely:

- Netting,
- Delivery versus payment, and
- Margin.

Specialized institutions involved in clearing and settlement that help reduce risks and lower costs are covered. These are:

- Registrars and transfer agents,
- Clearinghouses,
- Central depositories,
- Global custodians, and
- Communications networks.

1. Introduction

The way client funds are handled by brokers and others involved in the securities trading process is rarely discussed in financial markets courses, but this type of knowledge is essential for investors and financial professionals in modern capital markets. A prime example of why this knowledge is important is illustrated by the activities of Nick Leeson. Initially, Leeson made his name by solving clearing and settlement problems in Indonesia for Barings Bank. Barings, founded in 1762, was Britain's oldest merchant bank. Leeson was transferred to Barings's Singapore office, where he used his position as both office manager and the person in charge of clearing and settlement to hide 1.3 billion USD of trading losses. When the losses were finally exposed in 1995, the bank collapsed and Leeson was sent to jail. Potential problems with the way Barings had registered client accounts in Singapore raised questions about whether fund belonged to the bank and were subject to claims by creditors or were client funds. Similar issues arose in the bankruptcy of MF Global (see Box 4-1).

Box 4-1. The bankruptcy of MF Global

MF Global, a major derivatives broker, filed for bankruptcy protection on October 31, 2011. Investigations and subsequent developments revealed a number of problems. In the several days preceding the bankruptcy, the firm comingled customer money and firm money instead of segregating firm and customer money as required. Also, many clients of the firm had investments both within and outside the U.S. A trustee was appointed to oversee the liquidation of the firm's U.S. brokerage unit. One investor had deposits with the firm of 480,000 USD split equally between U.S. investments and investments outside the U.S. By May 2012 175,000 of his U.S. funds had been returned, but none of the funds invested outside the U.S. had been returned. KPMG insisted that it had the right to distribute the funds of an MF Global unit outside the U.S. under U.K. law. Customers stated that they had no idea that their recovery of funds from the U.S. firm could depend on whether they were trading U.S. or non-U.S. derivatives.

Source: For additional details see Lucchetti, Aaron, Customer divide at MF Global, Wall Street Journal, May 7, 2012, pp. C1, C2.

Clearing and settlement are an essential part of every securities transaction. In 1992 the Group of Thirty made nine recommendations concerning clearing and settlement of securities transactions (see Box 4-2).

These recommendations are still worth reviewing today as they embody a set of general principles related to clearing and settlement. [1] We will review these principals in this chapter. More and more investors are trading securities in multiple asset classes. There is also a trend toward trading in diverse locations and not just in the home market. Equities, fixed-income securities, and derivatives are often subject to different clearing and settlement procedures. Also, clearing and settlement requirements may

[1] In 1978 The Group of Thirty was established as a private, nonpartisan, nonprofit organization with the goal of deepening understanding of international economic and financial issues. The Group comprises 30 members who are senior representatives of the private and public sectors, including academics. Banks, corporations, foundations, central banks, and individuals provide support. http://www.group30.org/members.htm

Box 4-2: Group of Thirty recommendation on clearance and settlement of securities transactions

1. Trade comparison on T + 1. All comparisons of trades between direct market participants (brokers, dealers, other exchange members) should be accomplished by T + 1.

2. Trade comparisons for indirect participants. All indirect participants (institutions and other nonbroker/dealers) should be members of a system that achieves positive affirmation of trade details.

3. Central Depository. Each country should have an effective and fully developed central securities depository, organized and managed to encourage the broadest possible industry participation.

4. Netting. Each country should study its market and participation to determine whether trade-netting system would be beneficial in terms of reducing risk and promoting efficiency.

5. Delivery versus payment. Delivery versus payment should be employed as the method for settling all securities transactions.

6. Same day funds. Payments associated with the settlement of securities transactions and the servicing of securities portfolios should be consistent across all instruments and markets by adopting the 'same day' funds convention.

7. T + 3 rolling settlement. All markets should adopt a rolling settlement system. Final settlement should occur on T + 3.

8. Securities lending. Securities lending and borrowing should be encouraged as a method of expediting the settlement of securities transactions. Existing regulatory and taxation barriers that inhibit the practice of lending securities should be removed.

9. Use of ISO Standards 7775 and 6166. Each country should adopt the standard for securities messages developed by the International Organization for Standardization (ISO 7775). In particular, countries should adopt the ISIN numbering system for securities issues as defined in the ISO standard 6166, at least for cross border transactions.

Source: Group of Thirty, 1992, Clearance and Settlement Systems Status Report, Autumn, Washington. Reprinted by permission.

differ from one jurisdiction to another. Clearing and settlement are too important to be ignored by those dealing in financial markets today.

Broadly defined, the **clearing process** involves all the activities carried out from the time of a transaction until settlement. A crucial aspect of the clearing process is clearing, agreeing about the responsibilities of each party to a securities transaction. The details of each trade must be matched and agreed to by all parties, a process called trade comparison. Errors uncovered must be corrected. The clearing process may also involve the loaning of funds and securities, the posting of margin, and reporting details of the trade to counterparties, regulatory bodies, and exchanges. Settlement is the fulfillment of each party's obligation, which usually involves the transfer of financial instruments and funds.[1] An overview of clearing and settlement can be found in Rothwell (2007). Earlier sources include Parkinson et al. (1992) for the U.S. and The Bank for International Settlements (1992) for cross-border security settlement.

2. Types of risk

Clearing and settlement entail many risks.[2] While some risks are more important than others, an understanding of the various types of risk gives investors and securities industry professionals an appreciation of the obstacles and challenges faced in continuing to integrate across product types and across countries.

2.1. Credit risk

Credit risk is the risk that a transaction will never settle for full value.[3] Failure to settle due to economic reasons is a default. All counterparties to a

---

[1] Exchange web sites typically discuss the clearing and settlement process for that exchange. MBS Clearing Corporation provides clearing services for mortgage-backed securities to financial institutions in the US; its web address is http://www.mbscc.com/pmbscc1.htm.

[2] See Bank for International Settlements, November (1990) (the Lamfalussy Report) for a description of the first three types of risk discussed below.

[3] The Committee on Payment and Settlement Systems (CPSS) and the International Organization of Securities Commissions (IOSCO) have examined issues concerning the operation of securities settlement systems

trade face credit risk. Hence, firms need to monitor their level of exposure to each counterparty to make sure that a default will not jeopardize their survival. A default may have serious consequences because securities and funds that may be needed to fulfill obligations to other counterparties are not received. The credit risk that a firm faces due to a transaction has two components: replacement cost risk and principal risk.

2.1.1. Replacement cost risk

Counterparties are exposed to **replacement cost risk** if the value of the asset being exchanged at settlement changes between the time of the trade and settlement. If a firm's counterparty fails to deliver assets at settlement, the assets that are not delivered typically must be purchased in the open market so that the firm can make delivery to its own customers. Since most assets' prices fluctuate almost all trades are subject to replacement cost risk.

The replacement cost risk amount is the difference between the original trade price and the price that must be paid to purchase the assets from someone else. Suppose that a brokerage firm's client deposits 100 million USD and asks the firm to sell the USD for EUR. If the counterparty fails to deliver the EUR then the brokerage firm must buy the EUR from someone else so that it can fulfill its obligation to its client. Also, replacement cost risk is greater in a thin market than in a tick market. Replacement cost risk also is greater if a brokerage firm is representing a buyer in a bull market or a seller in a bear market.

Replacement cost risk is larger the longer the time between the transaction and its settlement and the greater the volatility of the assets traded. Replacement cost risk is typically small, but this is not always the case. During the week of October 6, 2008 the Standard and Poor's Index declined by more than 20% and, of course, many individual stocks had much greater declines. In recent years there have been more large returns that would be expected if returns are log normally distributed. If returns are log normally distributed, the October 1987 crash was a -27 standard

---

and the associated risk. These risks are summarized in the Disclosure Framework for Securities Settlement Systems, which is available at: http://www.bis.org/publ/cpss20.htm.

deviation event with a probability of 10^{-160} and the October 1989 crash was a -5 standard deviation event that should occur once every 14,756 years.[1]

2.1.2. Principal risk

Principal risk is the risk of loss resulting when one counterparty makes delivery, but, subsequently, the other counterparty fails to deliver. This is the most important type of credit risk because the entire value of the asset that has been delivered is at risk. Hence, principal risk can result in a greater loss than replacement cost risk. However, the duration of principal risk is typically much shorter than the duration of replacement cost risk. Recovering the assets that have been delivered may not be straightforward and can depend on the types of assets involved, regulations governing the counterparties, the location of the assets, and even the location of third parties.

2.2. Liquidity risk

Liquidity risk is the risk that a trade will settle for its full value, but after the agreed upon settlement time. Failure to settle on time results in a **failed transaction**. Liquidity risk can have serious consequences for a firm because, just like in the case of default, a firm whose counterparty does not deliver the expected assets on time must obtain these assets from another party. If the securities have been resold and substitute securities cannot be obtained quickly, a second failed transaction may occur. The brokerage firm representing the seller may have to borrow funds to pay its client. If interest rates are high, the cost of borrowing these funds may be high.

Financial institutions must maintain adequate credit and overdraft resources to prevent a failed transaction. If securities are delivered late in the day, an institution may not have adequate time to deliver them to the next party. Firms may be required to deliver assets before receiving funds to pay for the assets and vice versa.

---

[1] Jackwert and Rubinstein (1996) discuss the difficulties in analyzing return distributions caused by extreme outliers.

2.3. Operational risk

Operational risk is the risk that there will be a loss resulting from a failure of the hardware, software, communications, or others physical aspects involved in clearing and settlement. Events that might cause such a breakdown include fires, storms, earthquakes, power outages, and epidemics. However, the possibility of human error may also subject a firm to operational risk. In a well-known incident, in November 1985 when the Bank of New York began using a new internal clearing system for U.S. government securities the software had not been adequately tested under actual operating conditions and failed to operate properly. Consequently, payments were charged against the bank's account at the Federal Reserve, but no payments were credited because the bank could not send securities to other participants. Ultimately, the bank needed more than 20 billion USD of credit overnight to cover its overdraft.

Several incidents that were not directly involved in clearing and settlement nevertheless illustrate the potential for operational problems. At the opening of trading one day in December 1996, the Hong Kong Stock Exchange disseminated a large number of incorrect prices for the previous day's close. Many stocks were reported to have fallen by half and others to have more than doubled in price. Manual corrections were not completed until noon.[1] In June 2010 a quantitative hedge fund, AXA Rosenberg, announced that a coding error had affected the implementation of its investment strategy, but did not disclose the nature of the error. This problem is serious for a quantitative fund because buying and selling decisions are made by a computer. As a result of this error Charles Schwab closed four mutual funds run by AXA Rosenberg because it had lost confidence in the firm.[2]

---

[1] Wall Street Journal 1996, Hong Kong snafu tests investors' nerve, Wall Street Journal, December 13, 1996, pp. C1, C14.

[2] New York Times, June 20, 2010, p. 6.
http://www.nytimes.com/2010/06/20/business/20stra.html?_r=0

2.4. Systemic risk

According to the Group of Thirty, **systemic risk** is the risk that the failure of one counterparty to meet its obligations when due results in the inability of other counterparties to meet their obligations when due. If this definition is applied strictly, systemic risk is encountered frequently since the failure of a party to deliver securities needed for onward delivery is common. The topic of naked short sales has received considerable regulatory attention in recent years and has been banned in several countries. A naked short sale occurs when a trader makes a short sale without the intention of borrowing the stock for delivery.

However, most discussions of systemic risk focus on the occurrence of defaults and failed transactions that are so large that they cannot be managed and dealt with adequately using normal procedures, resulting is destabilization of the entire financial system. Numerous aspects of settlement systems expose the economy to systemic risk and the occurrence of what is sometimes referred to as a system meltdown. The size of financial transactions is typically large compared with participants' capital and payments, and receipts are not perfectly synchronized, resulting in very large exposure to principal risk. Further, information is limited. While a firm may know its own exposure to its counterparties the exposure of those counterparties to others will not typically be know. Hence, it is difficult for firms to protect themselves from this indirect exposure. An initial failed transaction or default will cause institutions to curtail their lending and slow their own settlements, putting downward pressure on prices and resulting in further defaults. This could lead to a vicious cycle of default begetting default.

In 1974 the medium-sized German bank, Bankhaus Herstatt, defaulted after the settlement of the DEM leg of its foreign exchange trades, but before the settlement of the USD leg. Counterparties that had made payments to Bankhaus Herstatt did not receive corresponding payments. Confidence in the settlement system was shaken and banks feared that other counterparties might also collapse. Several banks in New York refused to make payments on their own or customers' accounts until the situation clarified. As a result, for three days following the bankruptcy the daily value of gross funds transfers fell from 60 billion USD to about 36 billion USD. Restarting the system proved difficult.

The cross-currency settlement risk described in the previous paragraph is now known as **Herstatt risk**. Herstatt risk is important for foreign exchange trading because (1) foreign exchange transactions typically involve large sums, and (2) banks located in different time zones may not be open at the same time so that the two legs of a foreign exchange trade cannot be made simultaneously.

2.5. Errors risk

There are many ways to err in executing a trade including buying instead of selling or selling instead of buying, or trading the wrong asset or the wrong amount of an asset, trading at the wrong price, which could occur if a limit order was mistaken for a market order. All of these are examples of **errors risk. Fat finger trades** are erroneous trades entered by brokerage firm employees. The fact that computers now execute trades at a near speed-of-light pace may prevent the error from being discovered until it is too late.[1] In October 1998 the brokerage firm Salomon Brothers unintentionally sold 10,000 futures contracts on French government bonds on the French derivatives exchange Matif, losing several million USD when it had to buy them back. An audit revealed that the error was caused by a trader leaning his elbow on his computer keyboard's F12 button, which was programmed as the "instant sell" key. In another case, a Morgan Stanley trader entered an order to buy 100,000 units, failing to realize that the system he was using automatically multiplied orders by 1,000. What should have been an order worth 10.8 million EUR became an order for 10.8 billion EUR. About 81.5 million shares were traded before the bank

---

[1] Ishmael, Stacy-Marie, The curse of the fat-fingered trader, Financial Times (London). Posted by on Mar 16 16:12 provides a description of the ten most costly (or idiotic) errors of all time.

http://ftalphaville.ft.com/blog/2007/03/16/3207/the-curse-of-the-fat-fingered-trader/

cancelled the order. The error cost the bank 300,000 USD in fines plus trading losses.[1]

A trader placed an order to sell 1 million shares of Corinthian Colleges instead of the intended order of 100,000 shares. The stock price quickly dropped from about 57 USD to a low of 19 USD before trading was halted. More than 12 million shares had changed hands. Nasdaq subsequently cancelled all trades made between 10:46 am and 10:58 am.[2]

Straight through processing, which allows companies to transfer data about a transaction from one step in the clearing and settlement process to the next electronically without the need for manual manipulation, is designed to address the problem of fat fingers.

2.6. Other risk

Many types of organizations are involved in clearing and settlement including brokerage firms, clearinghouses, exchanges, and depositories. Any of these organizations could fail, resulting in substantial losses to those dealing with them. Both investors and financial institutions could face losses. The laws governing how losses will be apportioned if a failure occurs are typically not clear. If multiple jurisdictions are involved, which is likely, there may be conflicting laws, rules and interests. The collapse of Barings Bank described at the beginning of this chapter provides an example. Despite rules to the contrary, Barings Bank's accounts in Singapore did not distinguish between bank proprietary accounts and customer account. If the legal authorities in Singapore had decided not to allow the London bank to identify the actual owners of the funds, the customer funds potentially could have been used to compensate the bank's counterparties. There is no guarantee that officials in other countries will be equally protective of customer money, especially if that means local institutions would be

---

[1] Wilkinson, Tara Loader, The fat finger points to trouble for traders, Financial News, 14 Mar 2007.
http://www.efinancialnews.com/story/2007-03-14/the-fat-finger-points-to-trouble-for-traders-1

[2] Reiber, Beth Demain, Shares of Corinthian Colleges are halted after trading error. Wall Street Journal, December 8, 2003, p. C13.

subsidizing noncitizens. Moreover, the Barings case illustrates that the margins posted at the futures exchanges might not be sufficient in the case of a catastrophic loss.

MF Global, a major derivatives broker, filed for bankruptcy protection on October 31, 2011. Investigations and subsequent developments revealed a number of problems. In the several days preceding the bankruptcy, the firm comingled customer money and firm money instead of segregating firm and customer money as required. Also, many clients of the firm had investments both within and outside the U.S. A trustee was appointed to oversee the liquidation of the firm's U.S. brokerage unit. One investor had deposits with the firm of 480,000 USD split equally between U.S. investments and investments outside the U.S. By May 2012 175,000 of his U.S. funds had been returned, but none of the funds invested outside the U.S. had been returned. KPMG insisted that it had the right to distribute the funds of an MF Global unit outside the U.S. under U.K. law. Customers stated that they had no idea that their recovery of funds from the U.S. firm could depend on whether they were trading U.S. or non-U.S. derivatives.[1]

3. Techniques for dealing with risk

In this section we deal with three ways of conducting business that help mitigate clearing and settlement risk, namely, netting, delivery versus payment, and margin.

3.1. Netting

Netting is the offsetting of obligations by trading partners. Buys and sells of assets with the same counterparty are offset so that only the net amount of each asset and funds are transferred. This typically dramatically reduces the size of transfers, reducing settlement risk. Netting agreements specify the obligations of each party in the event of a default or failed transaction. Governments typically adopt laws that recognize that netting reduces each counterparty's obligation. In the absence of such recognition, in some

---

[1] Customer divide at MF Global, Wall Street Journal, May 7, 2012, pp. C1, C2.

jurisdictions, the administrator of a failed financial institution can choose to settle all profitable trades and repudiate unprofitable trades. From the non-failing counterparties' viewpoint, its profitable trades are not honored and it is obligated to settle it unprofitable trades. Counterparties to unprofitable trades might be low in the queue for receiving payment and, consequently, face high risk of partial or complete loss of principal. A legally enforceable netting agreement limits exposure.

Netting rules for trades in markets for traditional securities are typically well understood. However, as new securities are developed establishing netting rules, standard netting contracts, and ensuring that these are recognized by various jurisdictions is one of the first steps. Without a netting agreement the counterparty to the failing institution would have lost not only the gain on its profitable trades, but might also have been liable to pay any losses on its unprofitable trades with the failing institution.[1]

3.1.1. Bilateral netting

Bilateral netting is an agreement between two trading partners to exchange net amounts rather than gross amounts at settlement. **Novation** is the satisfaction and discharge of one contract by the substitution of a new contract. In the area of foreign exchange, **netting-by-novation** provides for the replacement of all agreements between two counterparties with a single agreement and individual single periodic payments. Running balances are maintained for each future value date. According to the Bank for International Settlements (1990, p. 11), "in some markets participants may be able to achieve a reduction of more than 50% in total payments to be made in all currencies, both in terms of value and volume." In the event of default the net exposure is the net present value of the running balance.

Master agreements such as the master agreement of the International Swap Dealers Association facilitate netting. A **master agreement** stipulates that individual transactions between counterparties are part of a single contractual relationship, which allows the netting of obligations upon bankruptcy and the netting of payments due on a specific date. However, despite the presence of a netting agreement, for swaps the individual

---

[1] Alron (1992), Glass (1994), and Hendricks (1994) examine issues related to netting.

transactions retain their separate terms, rates, and maturities and are implemented individually.

A simple bilateral example may be worthwhile. Suppose that one morning Firm X sells 42,000 shares of Firm A's common stock to Firm Y for 4.2 million EUR. Then, later in the day Firm Y sells 40,000 shares of Firm A's common stock to Firm X for 4 million EUR. If Firms X and Y have a netting agreement, on settlement day only the net amounts of shares and cash are exchanged. In this case, Firm Y would pay Firm X 0.2 million EUR and Firm X would provide Firm Y with 2,000 shares of Firm A's common stock. Thus, the replacement cost risk has been eliminated for Firm Y and has been reduced to 2,000 shares for Firm X. The credit risk is eliminated for Firm X and is reduced from 4.2 million EUR to 0.2 EUR for Firm Y.

3.1.2. Multilateral netting

Multilateral netting arrangements are common and multilateral netting can be achieved in several ways. In some markets, participants enter into individual transactions, and, if specified conditions are met, the clearinghouse is substituted a counterparty for both the buyer and the seller. In other systems the clearinghouse calculates a multilateral net position for each participant relative to other participants, but does not become counterparty to the transaction and provides no guarantee.

Payments between banks are typically netted so that only the net amount needs to be transferred. Sometimes once a transaction is cleared a central party is substituted for the individual parties and the original parties are released from any further obligation or risk. This is referred to as novation, which was discussed above. What happens in the case of default can vary. In some cases, the positions of the defaulting party are unwound and the settlement process is redone as if the defaulting party was not involved. This resolution can lead to defaults of other participants because they may have been counting on the funds or securities provided by the defaulting party to make their own settlements. Another possibility is that the central counterparty may guarantee performance and then allocate the loss among the participants based on total volume of transactions or volume of transactions with the counterparty. Using such a procedure everyone will share in the loss regardless of whether or not they traded with the defaulting counterparty.

Suppose that on a given day we have the following transactions:

(a) Bank X sells 1.5 million EUR to Bank Y for 1 million USD,

(b) Bank Y sells 3 million EUR to Bank Z for 2 million USD,

(c) Bank Z sells Bank Y 1.5 million EUR for 1 million USD.

Without netting, to settle these trades, each bank makes 2 payments (and receives two payments), for a total of 6 payments. With netting, as shown in Table 4-1, only two payments are required: Bank X pays bank Z 1.5 million EUR and Bank Z pays Bank X 1 million USD. Hence, multilateral netting can reduce credit and liquidity risk substantially. Note that here, if the netting arrangements are final and not subject to revocation, the risk of Bank Y is totally eliminated. Also although Banks X and Z did not trade with each other, they are exchanging payments. If a default occurs, there is exposure to parties with whom one has not dealt directly.

Table 4-1. Multilateral netting example

	Bank X		**Bank Y**		**Bank Z**	
	EUR	USD	EUR	USD	EUR	USD
Trade			Cash flows			
(a)	+1.5	-1	-1.5	+1		
(b)	-3	+2			+3	-2
(c)			+1.5	-1	-1.5	+1
Net	-1.5	+1	0	0	+1.5	-1

Note: all numbers in millions.

Source: Prepared by authors.

3.1.3. Real time gross settlement

A new trend in settlement made possible by the speed and reliability of modern communications is **real time gross settlement.** Under this system fund transfers from one bank to another take place on a gross basis in real time without any netting. Settlement is not subject to any waiting period and, once processed, payments are final and irrevocable. This type of payment system is maintained by the central banks of the 26 members of the European Union. Credit risk resulting from settlement lags due to waiting until the end of the day to settle is eliminated. This type of payment system is most suitable when the volume of payments is low and the value is high.

3.2. Settlement day and delivery versus payment

Securities markets have been working to reduce replacement cost risk and principal risk for many years. Efforts to reduce replacement cost risk have focused on reducing the difference between the trade time and settlement time. A key to reducing principal risk is achieving **delivery versus payment**, which means that the two legs of a settlement occur simultaneously. The Bank for International Settlements (1992) provides a discussion of delivery versus payment.

3.2.1. Settlement day—securities and derivatives

Historically, the delay between clearing and settlement followed a variety of patterns. In some markets, historically, transactions over a period of time were accumulated and settled at the same time. Trades on the London Stock Exchange were divided into trading accounts typically of two weeks duration. All trades during one trading account were settled on the account day, usually the second Monday after the end of the account. Transactions on the Milan Stock Exchange were settled on the final day of each calendar month and refer to the previous trading interval that runs from mid-month to mid-month.

In contrast, **rolling settlement** involves settling all the trades on a given day on a designated subsequent day. The U.S. used rolling settlement of T + 5 for securities for many years. T represents the transactions day and +5 means five business days after the transactions day. However, India was only able to introduce T + 5 settlement in 1999.

The Group of Thirty recommended that equities settlement be for T + 3 and this is the practice now followed in most countries. For purchases on Mondays, if there is no holiday, payment is due Thursday. Since Saturday and Sunday are not working days in the U.S., a trade on Friday would be settled on Wednesday. This type of settlement is **regular way** in the U.S.

Many securities markets also have arrangements for alternate settlements.[1] For example, in the U.S., trades can be arranged for **cash** settlement in which payments are made and the financial instrument is delivered on the day of the transaction. However, trades for cash are used only in unusual circumstances because of their high cost.

For exchange-traded derivatives including futures contracts, margin must typically be posted before the opening of trading on the next business day. Options are settled on T + 1. Because of their higher level of risk, settlement times for derivatives have historically been short. These short settlement times are feasible because the ownership records of derivatives are electronic and not in physical form.

The Group of Thirty has recommended the use of same day funds for payments involving financial instruments. If both funds and securities are in electronic form, both can be exchanged between brokerage firms and final customers on settlement day. But if physical certificates are used settlement is more cumbersome. Suppose that the seller is required to deliver the certificate to the seller's brokerage firm on T + 5. The buying firm then sends the certificate to the transfer agent (discussed below) to check the documents to make sure that they are in **good order**, which means that they meet all legal requirements, and for issuing a new certificate. The transfer agent must make sure that the new certificate is for the same number of shares as the old certificate. The transfer agent records the transaction and sends both the old and new certificates to the registrar. The registrar (discussed below) checks that the number of shares received by the new owner equals the number of shares supplied by the old owner. In some jurisdictions, the registrar and transfer agent can be the same firm or the firms can serve as registrar for their own shares. If a new certificate is issued, the transfer agent sends the certificate directly to the customer or to the customer's broker to be resent to the customer. All these steps could

---

[1] According to Bonte-Friedheim (1996) when the governor of the central bank of Kenya asked, the head of Barings Asset Management, Michael Power, for suggestions on how to entice more foreign investors to Kenya Power suggested speeding up settlement system so that investors did not have to wait six weeks to be paid.

extend over several weeks depending on the location of each party in relation to the others.

Settlement date is the date on which the purchaser owns the securities and the seller is entitled to receive the sales proceeds. Companies that pay dividends announce the dividend on the **declaration date**. The announcement of the dividend contains two dates. The **record date** is the day on which an investor must own the stock to be entitled to the dividend. The **payment date** is the date that a firm actually pays a dividend. The **ex-dividend** date is the day on and after which a purchaser of stock is not entitled to the dividend. Suppose that a market center settles on TD + 3. Denote the record date as RD. Consider a trade on RD – 3. In this case TD = RD - 3 so that settlement is on TD + 3 = RD. Since the settlement day is on the record day, the purchaser would receive the dividend. On the other hand, a trade on RD – 2 would settle on RD + 1 and would not receive the dividend. Hence, the ex-dividend date is two business days prior to the record date. On the ex-dividend date, *ceteris paribus*, the firm's stock price will fall by the amount of the dividend.

3.2.2. Settlement day—currencies

For most currencies traded against the USD, including the EUR and the JPY, the settlement day is the second business day after the trade. This two-day period gives the parties time to process the trade. However, for MXP and CAD trades against the USD, settlement is the next business day. **Value date** is another name for the settlement date. The **dealing locations** are the countries of the counterparties. Settlement takes place in the country whose currency is involved. In other words, in a trade of JPY against USD, the payment of JPY is made in Japan and the payment of USD is made in the U.S. **Settlement locations** depend on the currencies involved, not on the location of the parties to the trade.

For currencies that settle in two business days, if the first business day following a trade is a holiday in one settlement location, but not in the other, when is the settlement date? Typically, in the absence of special arrangements, the settlement date is the date of the liquidity provider rather than the liquidity demander. So if Bank A calls Bank B to initiate a trade, then, the value date of Bank B applies. Note that in this case the issue of holidays is relative to the dealing locations because the counterparties need sufficient time to process the trades. The principal of delivery-versus-payment suggests that both counterparties settle on the same day. If the appropriate settlement day is a holiday in either settlement location or in either dealing location, the settlement is postponed to the next business day. Suppose that U.S. and British banks consummate a USD/GBP trade on Friday. Banks in London and New York are closed on Saturdays and Sundays so that a trade on Friday ordinarily settles on the following Tuesday. If the following Tuesday is a holiday in either the U.S. or the U.K., settlement is postponed until Wednesday. Further, suppose that a USD/GBP trade consummated by a Singapore bank and a Japanese bank is due to settle on Wednesday, but Wednesday is a holiday in either the U.S. or U.K. Then, if Thursday is not a holiday settlement will be postponed until that day. In this case the value date is affected by holidays in the settlement location rather than in the dealing location.

Settlements of Middle Eastern currencies are a special case because Islamic banks are closed on Friday but open on Saturday and Sunday. A trade on a Wednesday of USDs against a Middle Eastern currency would normally be on T + 2 or Friday. However, Middle Eastern banks are closed on Friday so that the delivery cannot take place. Instead, only the USD is delivered on Friday and the Middle Eastern currency is delivered on Saturday.

3.3. Risk control strategies

Clearinghouses, central depositories and other organizations involved in clearing and settlement (discussed below) do not entirely eliminate risk. On October 1987 during the Asian currency crisis many brokers on the Hong Kong Futures Exchange were unable to meet their margin calls. Consequently, the Hong Kong Futures Guarantee Corporation, which guaranteed all the contracts, faced bankruptcy. In order to prevent Hong Kong from having the first futures exchange to fail, the Honk Kong government stepped in an arranged rescue funding.[1] In another case, in

---

[1] For additional discussion of this topic see: http://www.numa.com/derivs/ref/c-risk/cr-hk.htm.

1995 thieves accessed the accounts of three investment funds at the depository of the Czech Republic and stole more than 15 million USD of securities.[1] In the U.S. individual brokerage accounts are protected against a broker's default by the Security Investors Protection Corporation within limits (500,000 USD per customer, 100,000 USD for cash).

In the remainder of this section, we discuss various ways that are used to reduce risk from the failure of clearinghouses and others involved in the clearing and settlement process. Approaches for reducing risk include limiting membership and establishing credit limits, margin, and developing systems for risk monitoring and control.

Participants in the clearing and settlement process are typically screened so that only those that are credit worthy can participate. However, passing the initial screen is just the first step. Each participant's net debit position is likely to be limited according to its credit worthiness. However, the procedures should be fair and "the methods and criteria used to limit participation should be as objective as possible and not based on a desire to maintain the competitive advantages of some market players."[2] If the participant's limit is reached no further debit trades can be processed until additional collateral is supplied. However, this approach can result in failed transactions.

Clearinghouses usually try to minimize failed transactions. One way to do this is by having multiple cycles in the clearing process (perhaps by operating both day and night). If a transaction cannot be processed in one cycle participants can submit additional securities or collateral so that the trade can settle in the next round.

In addition to creditworthiness, affirmative steps to ensure ability to pay may be required. Exchanges and clearinghouses can establish guarantee funds. However, these funds typically protect other members, not the clients of members. Also, in some cases bank letters of credit may be required. Yet there is substantial risk that in the event of default the credit line will be withdrawn.

Another approach is requiring margin. **Margin** has different meanings. Here we focus on margin that is used to provide a buffer or cushion to

---

[1] Sesit (1997).

[2] IOSCO, 1992, p. 21.

provide protection in the settlement process. Brokers often must deposit margin with exchanges or clearinghouses to guarantee performance on contracts. Also, brokers may post margin so that the clearinghouse has a fund available to deal with a default by a participant or member.

Clearinghouses choose the types of collateral they accept. All take cash in local currency and government securities. However, some also take equities and bonds some of which may be denominated in non-domestic currencies. The clearinghouses apply haircuts to the non-cash and non-government bond collateral based on the riskiness of the collateral. The frequency with which they reevaluate the size of the haircut or the adequacy of the collateral varies. In some cases the collateral may not be fully paid but represent a pledge such as in the form of a letter of credit. The Options Clearing Corporation has a 3.5 billion USD guarantee fund and an 'AAA' credit rating.

Cross margining permits netting of gains and losses across different product types or even different markets such as cash and derivatives. The number of markets and instruments eligible for cross margining in the U.S. has grown markedly. The Options Clearing Corporation (OCC) introduced cross margining in 1989. Cross margining is available when products in different markets are cleared by the OCC as well as those cleared by the Chicago Mercantile Exchange and ICE Clear US. Cross margining was designed for firms with memberships in multiple clearing organizations and trading products with highly-correlated prices. Cross margining is only available to clearing members and their affiliates, and market professionals (market makers and futures locals).

Individuals also must deposit margin with their brokers to guarantee performance on futures contracts. In some cases these margins are redeposited with the clearinghouse, but in other cases the broker is only required to post margin after netting long and short positions. Margins for futures are considered performance guarantees. Exchanges establish margin requirements based on the volatility of the underlying assets. Margin can usually be posted in either cash or acceptable securities such as U.S. Treasury bills.

Risk monitoring and control is the use of sophisticated computer systems to track and limit the exposure of participants to risk. The International Organization of Securities Commissions (IOSCO) recommends this risk reduction strategy. An example of a comprehensive program for risk monitoring and control is the Theoretical Intermarket Margin System (TIMS) used by The Options Clearing Corporation. TIMS incorporates a sophisticated option pricing model, allows the stress testing of portfolios, takes implied volatility into account, and recognizes the benefits of portfolio diversification.

4. Institutions for dealing with risk

A number of institutional arrangements have been developed to deal with clearing and settlement. The most prominent of these are clearinghouses, central depositories, and communications networks.

4.1 Registrars and transfer agents

Publicly traded companies typically employ two entities—the **registrar** and **transfer agent**—to help in the management of shareholder accounts. We will consider each of these financial institutions in turn. The issuer sometimes performs the registrar function. In 1971 the NYSE began allowing a single financial institution (other than the issuer) to serve as both transfer agent and registrar. A registrar may be needed for both stock and bond issues.

When shares are traded or ownership changes for other reasons such as reorganizations or the death of the owner, if the shares are registered in the name of the seller, the certificate representing ownership must be cancelled and a new certificate issued. The registrar is charged with monitoring the issuance and cancellation of all of these certificates to ensure that the amount outstanding conforms exactly to that authorized so that an **out-of-proof** or **out-of-balance** condition does not exist.

The issuance of new certificates and the cancellation of old certificates is typically initiated by a financial institution known as a transfer agent. Besides the sale of shares to a new owner, ownership may change due to reorganization, merger or other corporate events. New shares may also results from stock dividends, stock splits and dividend reinvestment programs. Moreover, lost certificates may need to be replaced, which can be expensive, costing several percent of the value of the securities. The transfer agent keeps a record of who owns a company's stocks and bonds and whether the ownership is in book-entry form, a certificate has been issued to the owner, or the shares are held in **street name**. Street name indicates that ownership is recorded in the name of a financial institution such as a brokerage firm rather than in the name of the beneficial owner. The brokerage firm may, in turn, turn over the certificate to a depository. Transfer agents may also act as company representatives distributing dividends, proxies and other types of corporate communications such as quarterly and annual reports.

There are many financial institutions that act as transfer agents and registrars and some of these belong to the Securities Transfer Association, Inc.[1] Computershare, a publicly held company based in Australia, is currently the world's only global share registrar with over 61 million shareholder accounts. Computershare also provides transfer agent services for more than 2,700 public corporations with more than 17 million active shareholder accounts.[2] First American Stock Transfer, Inc. is an example of a smaller transfer agent.[3]

4.2. Clearinghouses

A **clearinghouse** is involved in clearing and settlement. The Options Clearing Corporation was founded in 1973 and is the world's largest equity options and futures clearinghouse.[4] In some cases organizations provide multiple services. For example, Clearstream, the clearing and settlement arm of Deutsche Borse Group, state that it is a leading European supplier of post-trading services. It was created in 2000 through the merger of Cedel International and Deutsche Borse Clearing. Clearstream handled 114

---

[1] http://www.stai.org/index.php

[2] http://www-us.computershare.com/Default.asp?cc=US&lang=EN

[3] http://www.firstamericanstock.com/

[4] According to the OCC's web site: Participant exchanges include: BATS, Chicago Board Options Exchange, International Securities Exchange, NASDAQ OMX BX, Inc., NASDAQ OMX PHLX, Nasdaq Stock Market, NYSE Amex, and NYSE Arca. Our clearing members serve both professional traders and public customers and comprise approximately 120 of the largest U.S. broker-dealers.

million transactions, and was custodian of securities worth 10.6 trillion EUR (Deutsche Borse Annual Report, 2008).[1] LCH.Clearnet, which is the leading independent clearinghouse, serves major international exchanges and platforms, including OTC markets, and clears a variety of asset classes such as securities (both equities and bonds), exchange traded derivatives, energy, freight, interbank interest rate swaps credit derivative swaps, and euro and sterling denominated bonds and repos.[2]

Following the economic crisis of 2008 there has been an interested push by regulators to use clearinghouses to clear over-the-counter trades. The primary motivation is to protect counterparties from credit risk and thereby reduce systemic risk.[3] LCH.Clearnet substantially expanded its operations. The firm, which began clearing plain vanilla interest rate swaps in four major currencies in 1999, cleared swaps in 17 currencies, representing more than 50% of the interested rate swaps market in 2012. In 2012 the notional value of assets cleared was over 340 trillion USD with another 140 trillion USD of cleared transactions removed through trade comparisons.[4] ICE Clear Credit was established in 2009 and in 2013 is the world's largest clearinghouse for credit default swaps.[5]

One of the most important functions of a clearinghouse is to reduce risk by guaranteeing performance on contracts typically through novation.[6] A **clearing member** is a direct participant in a clearinghouse and is typically limited to firms with strong financial positions. Smaller firms and those

---

[1] http://www.clearstream.com/ci/dispatch/en/kir/ci_nav/home

[2] http://www.lchclearnet.com/

[3] Grant, Jeremy, Clearing up the system, Financial Times, November 2, 2009m p. 11.

[4] http://www.lchclearnet.com/swaps/swapclear_for_clearing_members/

[5] https://www.theice.com/clear_credit.jhtml

[6] As a clearing house, LCH.Clearnet sits in the middle of a trade, assuming the counterparty risk .... When the trade is registered with LCH.Clearnet, it becomes the legal counterparty to the trade, ensuring the financial performance; if one of the parties fails, LCH.Clearnet steps in. By assuming the counterparty risk, LCH.Clearnet underpins many important financial markets, facilitating trading and increasing confidence within the market. http://www.lchclearnet.com/about_us/

with lesser credit standing must deal with the clearinghouse through the clearing members.

Some clearinghouses provide trade comparison services. As mentioned above, trade comparison is the process of matching and confirming the terms of a trade, including the identity of the counterparties and the asset, the price and quantity, and whether there are special terms. The National Securities Clearing Corporation provides trade comparison services for U.S. equities and corporate and municipal bonds.[1] The National Securities Clearing Corporation also performs multilateral netting.[2]

4.3. Central depositories

A **central depository** is an organization that accepts deposits of securities and that accounts for transfers of these securities among participants.[3] Historically, owners of stock received a **stock certificate,** which was the physical evidence of their ownership. In January 2009 the Japanese

---

[1] Other Clearing Organizations include the Government Securities Clearing Corp., the Mortgage Backed Securities Clearing Corp., and the International Securities Clearing Corp.
http://financial-dictionary.thefreedictionary.com/National+Securities+Clearing+Corporation

[2] As pointed out at http://www.numa.com/derivs/ref/c-risk/cr-hk.htm, clearing arrangements vary widely. In some cases the clearing entity is an integral part of the exchange (such as the Osaka Stock Exchange) or a subsidiary of the exchange (as is the case for Deutsche Borse Group), or it may be a completely separate institution (for example, the LCH.Clearnet).

[3] CDS Clearing and Depository Services Inc. supports Canada's equity, fixed income and money markets, holding over $3 trillion on deposit and handling over 251 million domestic trades annually. CDS is accountable for the safe custody and movement of securities, accurate record keeping, the processing of post-trade transactions, and the collection and distribution of entitlements relating to the securities that have been deposited by participants. Its web site is:
http://www.cds.ca/cdsclearinghome.nsf/Pages/-EN-Profile?Open.

Securities Depository Center (JASDEC) established a new system of book entry or **dematerialized** ownership records.[1] In some countries there are multiple depositories dealing with different types of securities or particular groups of institutions and brokerage firms.[2] There are two depositories in India.

If they continue to exist, physical certificates evidencing ownership can be **immobilized** and stored in a central vault of a depository to eliminate physical movements of the certificates when ownership changes. Certificates are deposited and a book-entry account is created showing the participant's ownership position. The process is reversed if shares are withdrawn from the depository. The physical certificate is held by the depositary in its name. Settlement involves transferring entries on the books of the depositary. The ownership records are **dematerialized** if the certificates cease to exist so that all ownership records are in electronic form. Examples of countries with dematerialized equities are Singapore, Israel, and India. In India it is possible to go through a process called **rematerialization** to get securities in an electronic form converted back into the physical form. U.S. government treasury securities and most derivatives are dematerialized in the US.

A depository reduces costs and risks of transfers. Eliminating the printing of new certificates and the physical movement of certificates each time there is a change in ownership reduces costs. Risk of loss due to forgery and losses of certificates are also eliminated.

In 1995, the National Securities Clearing Corporation Limited was established as a subsidiary of National Stock Exchange of India to provide clearing and settlement services for equities and derivatives. This was India's first depositary. A related organization was established the following year to provide clearing and settlement services for government securities and for other markets such as the Over the Counter Exchange of India (OTCEI). Previously, clearing and settlement in India illustrated the worse aspects of a physical settlement system. In some cases transfer of a physical

---

[1] For additional information see: http://www.jasdec.com/download/annual_r/ar2009_06.pdf.

[2] One US depository is The Depository Trust Company whose web address is: http://www.dtc.org/in/.

certificate could require scores or even more than 100 signatures. Registrars rejected ten to fifteen percent of certificates submitted due to mistakes. Security was lax and certificates were stored in a trailer by one Indian bank.[1] In 1997 the Securities and Exchange Board of India[2] ordered institutional investors to use the country's electronic share depository and the process of dematerializing certificates began.

In Singapore, accounts at the Central Depository are in the names of individuals so that an individual can easily deal with more than one brokerage firm. When shares are bought the brokerage firm simply has the Central Depository credit these shares to the customer's account. When the shares are sold the brokerage firm has the customer's account debited for the shares. There is no need for the same brokerage firm to be used in buying and selling the shares. In contrast, U.S. brokerage firms have vigorously opposed the establishment of individual accounts in the U.S. Instead, these brokerage firms advocate having one or more central depositories with only institutional accounts allowed. The individual brokerage firms would then maintain their own customer accounts. Restrictions on individual accounts at the central depository make the use of one brokerage firm for buying and another for selling more difficult, which, of course, is the brokers aim.

In many markets certificates exist in both registered and bearer form. **Registered** means that the identity of the owner is recorded on the books of the registrar. **Bearer** securities are negotiable upon delivery and physical (or book-entry) possession is all that is required to effect ownership changes. The security requirements for bearer certificates are much higher than for registered certificates and some central depositories do not accept bearer certificates.

---

[1] Karp 1997, Karp and Sharma (1997) and Sesit (1997).

[2] For additional information see the Board's web site: http://www.sebi.com/.

4.4 Global custodians

Global custodians are financial institutions that ensure that clients' financial transactions are settled properly and registered correctly.[1] They also protect the ownership rights of their clients including protection in such matters as dividends, stock splits and voting. Investors may also rely on custodians to know which brokers can be trusted. While developed markets have well understood rules, the laws in emerging markets may not even recognize private ownership. In 1997 one custodian refused to do custodial work in Russia unless the client signed a statement acknowledging the risks. Hermitage Capital Management has "been involved in 38 Russian court cases and lost 36 of them. Many of the decisions were clearly irrational. It is particularly apparent when you look at our experience in courts outside of Russia where we have a 66% success rate, versus a 95% loss rate inside the country. Basically, we have come to the conclusion that one can hardly get a fair trial in courts in Russia."[2]

4.5. Communication networks

Financial markets rely on communication to execute trades and also to implement clearing and settlement. The importance of communications is illustrated by Warf (1989) who shows the explosive growth of expenditures on telecommunications by securities firms in recent years. McPartland, Taylor, and Pozdena (1989) state that "even in the derivatives markets, where there are fewer obstacles to the development of a 24-hour system, a switch to round-the-clock trading would still bring that market up against a powerful stumbling block: the lack of a 24-hour-a-day payment system offering finality of settlement." The Society for Worldwide Interbank

---

[1] Examples of global custodians include: Brown Brothers Harriman & Co., http://www.bbh.com/general/brochure.htm; Lloyds Bank Securities Services,
http://www.custody.lloyds-bank.co.uk/index.html; and Standard Chartered (Singapore), http://www.globewatch.com/eq/index.html.

[2]
http://hermitagefund.com/newsandmedia/index.php?ELEMENT_ID=246

Financial Telecommunications (SWIFT) is probably the most important international network. Another important network is the Clearing House Interbank Payments System (CHIPS) in the U.S. We describe each of these, in turn.

4.5.1. SWIFT

SWIFT operates 24/7 and supplies highly secure and reliable communications services to more than 9,000 financial institutions, such as banks, securities firms and other corporations institutions and corporate customers in more than 200 countries (as of 2010). However, SWIFT does not participate directly in funds transfers or in clearing and settlement except by relaying messages.

SWIFT is owned by its member banks and shares allocated primarily based on usage.[1] These shareholder banks are known as members. SWIFT users exchange millions of messages a day involving trillions of USD of transactions. The breakdown of SWIFT message volume (in millions) by type during 2008 was: payments, 1908; securities, 1,626; treasury, 261; trade, 46; and system 14. Securities traffic has the highest rate of growth.

SWIFT has been the global leader in providing telecommunications technology for automated cross-border payments. Users seek ease of use, reliability, and standardized information that meet accounting and regulatory needs. SWIFT insures reliability and security by checking the identity of the sender, the format of the message, acknowledging the message's acceptance by the system only if it conforms, encrypting the message during transit and storage, and guaranteeing delivery of the message.

4.5.2. CHIPS and Fedwire

The **Clearing House Interbank Payments System (CHIPS),** established in 1853, was the first and is now the largest bank clearinghouse. CHIPS is the leader in clearing and settling USD payments, handling 95% of all USD payments worldwide. Services are provided for checks, wire

---

[1] The average daily value of payments messages is more than 2 trillion USD. SWIFT 's site is: http://www.swift.com/.

transfers and other payment types. CHIPS was established by The New York Clearing House Association.[1] CHIPS maintains a hot backup facility so that it can relocate its operations in five minutes in case of a disaster. Only the largest banks use CHIPS. On a typical day substantially more than $1 trillion USD in payments clears through CHIPS. The number of transactions is about 200,000 daily. CHIPS is owned by its participating banks. CHIPS nets payments so that settlement is not in real time. Note that CHIPS payments executed throughout the day are irrevocable and are paid through settlement at the end of the day.

The U.S. Federal Reserve Banks operate the **Federal Reserve Wire Network (Fedwire).** Fedwire is a real time gross settlement system that allows the electronic transfer of USD funds among more than 9,000 participants. Payment over Fedwire average about 3 trillion USD a day, representing more than 500,000 transactions.[2]

5. Summary

This chapter describes clearing, the process by which counterparties agree on the terms of a trade, and settlement, the process of fulfilling the terms of the trade. There are many risks associated with clearing and settlement. Parties to a trade face credit risk, the risk that a trade will not settle for full value. If one party settles and the other does not, the party settling could potentially lose the entire value of the assets in the trade, which is called principal risk. If both parties do not settle, each party risks loss of the difference between the trade price and the price at the time of failure to

---

[1] The oldest clearinghouse in the United States, The New York Clearing House simplified the exchange of checks and improved the efficiency of the payments process. The NYCH has never failed to settle. CHIPS settles over 1 trillion USD a day, representing more than 250,000 transactions. For additional information see: http://theclearinghouse.org/home.php.

[2] Similar payment systems exist in many countries. The GIRO system in Singapore allows brokerage firms to directly debit or credit individuals' bank accounts.

http://www.abs.org.sg/cms/index.php?option=com_content&task=view&id=46&Itemid=102other)

settle. This is called replacement cost risk. Parties face liquidity risk, the risk that a trade will settle for full value, but after the agreed upon time. There have been many instances in which computers systems have gone down, software has not worked as expected, or communications systems have failed. Because of the myriad of risks faced in clearing and settlement, a number of ways of mitigating these risks have been developed. First, there are ways of going about the clearing and settlement process that can reduce risk. Rather that exchanging the assets and funds involved in a trade, counterparties can exchange only the assets and funds resulting from many trades. This process, called netting greatly reduces the value of the assets actually exchanged and, therefore, reduces risk. Netting can be bilateral between two parties, or multilateral between multiple parties. Another ways to reduce is through delivery versus payment, which means that the counterparties all exchange assets at the same time. Finally, margin can be posted to insure performance at settlement. The financial institutions involved in clearing and settlement described next often collect margin.

Secondly, a number of financial institutions have been created to mitigate the risks of clearing and settlement. Registrars and transfer agents make sure that the records of ownership are updated following a trade. Clearinghouses are involved in the actual process of clearing and settlement among counterparties. Often during the clearing process the clearinghouse will interpose itself as the counterparty to each party to a trade. In this case, each counterparty looks to the clearinghouse at settlement. Depositories facilitate settlement by reducing the need to exchange physical assets at settlement. Instead, settlement is made by book entry on the records of the depository. Global custodians perform many services for traders, including holding assets in multiple countries, collecting dividends, and arranging for voting in shareholder matters. Because of their familiarity with each local market, global custodians reduce the risk that investors would have in dealing with strangers.

Questions

1. Do clearing and settlement happen simultaneously?
2. List several ways to mitigate clearing and settlement problems.

3. Why is knowledge of clearing and settlement methods and institutions more important for those investing internationally?
4. Besides the increasing use of computers, name two other changes in practices that have improved clearing and settlement.
5. What are the obstacles to achieving perfect delivery versus payment?
6. What problems might arise if an earthquake destroyed a central depository's computer?

References

Alton, Gilbert R., 1992, Implications of netting arrangements for bank risk in foreign exchange transactions, Federal Reserve Bank of St. Louis Review 74, 3-16.

Bank for International Settlements, 1990, Report of the committee on interbank netting schemes of the central banks of the Group of Ten countries, Basle. (Lamfalussy Report).

Bank for International Settlements, 1992, Delivery versus payment in securities settlements systems, Basle.

Bank for International Settlements, 1995, Cross-border securities settlements, Basle.

Bonte-Friedheim, Robert, The treasure hunters: On the fringe: Fund managers flock to tiny stock markets that aren't hot yet, Wall Street Journal, November 13, 1996, A8.

Cooper, Ian A., and Antonio S. Mello, 1995, Netting and the design of financial contracts with default risk, Working paper, London Business School, London.

Edwards, Ben, 1994, Euroclear: Morgan's magic circle, Euromoney, August, pp. 35-38.

Glass, Garrett R., 1994, A primer on netting, Journal of Commercial Bank Lending 77, 18-25.

Group of Thirty, 1992, Clearance and Settlement Systems Status Report, Autumn, Washington.

Hendricks, Darryll, 1994, Netting agreements and the credit exposures of OTC derivatives portfolios, Federal Reserve Bank of New York Economic Policy Review 19, 7-18.

International Organization of Securities Commissions (IOSCO), 1992, Clearing and Settlement in Emerging Markets: A Blueprint, Montreal.

Jackwerth, Jens Carsten, and Mark Rubinstein, 1996, Recovering probability distributions from option prices, Journal of Finance 51, 1611-1631.

Karp, Jonathan, 1997, India: settlement problems, while still a nightmare are showing definite signs of improvement, Wall Street Journal, June 26, p. R14.

Karp, Jonathan, and Sumit Sharma, 1997, Paper chase ends as Indian stocks go electronic, Wall Street Journal, October 17, p. A14.

Loader, David, 2005, Clearing and Settlement in Derivatives. Butterworth-Heinemann.

McPartland, John, Kim Taylor, and Randall Pozdena, 1989, Extended hour trading, summary in, U.S. Congress, Office of Technology Assessment, Study of International Clearing and Settlement—volume I (PB91 127 54B), p. 184.

The Options Clearing Corporation, n.d., Theoretical intermarket margin system, Chicago.

Organization for Economic Co-operation and Development, 1991, Systemic Risk In Securities Markets, Paris.

Parkinson, Patrick, Adam Gilbert, Emily Gollob, Lauren Hargraves, Richard Mead, Jeff Stehm, and Mary Ann Taylor, 1992, Clearance and Settlement in U.S. Securities Markets, Board of Governors of the Federal Reserve System, Washington. (Provides an excellent, but dated, discussion of clearing and settlement in the US.)

Rothwell, Kevin, 2007, Handbook of Investment Administration. Securities and Investment Institute. Wiley: West Sussex, England.

Standard and Poor's, 2012, Margin for error; why all clearinghouse collateral is not created equal, online, 18-Dec-2012,

http://www.standardandpoors.com/ratings/articles/en/us/?articleType=HTML&assetID=1245346070203

Sesit, Michael R., 1997, Unsettled: Custodial services are taken for granted in most developed countries: not in emerging markets, Wall Street Journal, June 26, p. R6.

U.S. Congress, Office of Technology Assessment, 1989, Study of international clearing and settlement—volume I, VI (PB91 127 54B), p. 184.

Warf, Barney, 1989, Telecommunications and the globalization of communications services, Professional Geographer 41, 257-271.

CHAPTER FIVE

REGULATION

Key Terms

Absolute priority rule—each senior class of creditors receives full payment before any junior class or equity holders receive any payments.

Automatic stay—the filing of a bankruptcy petition automatically prevents creditors from enforcing their claims.

Bankruptcy—A legal process in which an organization is either liquidated or financially restructured and a court can often cancel debt.

Best execution—the requirement that a broker execute a trade in such a way that the client receives the best terms.

Blue sky laws—state laws in the U.S. regulating the sale of securities within the state.

Central bank—an organization that performs functions typically including creating money, serving as a lender of last resort, and acting as the government's fiscal agent.

Churning (by a broker)—excessive trading which benefits the broker by generating increased commissions without commensurate benefits for the client.

Churning (manipulation)—see painting the tape.

Cramdown—a bankruptcy plan that is forced on one or more groups of creditors.

Credit union—a financial institution created by and owned and controlled by its members, the individuals who use its services.

Debtor-in-possession—the case in which the existing board of directors is permitted to retain control of the assets of a firm after the filing of a bankruptcy petition.

Defined benefit plans—a type of pension benefit in which the payment of a specific sum is guarantee.

Defined contribution plans—a type of pension plan in which the participant's contributions rather than benefits are specified.

Direct investment—one firm either starts a new firm or purchases an existing firm.

Disclosure regulation—a type of regulation that requires individuals and firms with a fiduciary relationship publicize information pertinent to making investment decisions.

Efficient market—a market with reasonable prices for assets and reasonable costs of trading.

Employee Retirement Income Security Act (ERISA)—a U.S. law governing the administration of private pension plans.

Ethics—rules of conduct recognized as appropriate for a given set of relationships.

Fair market—a market that is free of deceptive and abusive practices and in which all participants have an opportunity to trade at the best price available for their size.

Federal Sentencing Guidelines for Organizations (U.S.)—guidelines established by the U.S. Sentencing Commission to foster uniform sentencing.

Financial Industry Regulatory Authority (FINA)—an independent regulator for all securities firms doing business in the U.S.

Foreign Corrupt Practices Act—a U.S. law that prohibits bribery to obtain or retain business.

Frontrunning—trading ahead of client orders by brokers.

Hawala networks—a system of brokers who transfer money without actually moving the money establishing a lender-debtor relation between the brokers.

Herstatt risk—see systemic risk.

Illegal insider trading—the use of information gained in a fiduciary relationship to make trading profits.

Information efficiency—everyone has the same beliefs and information so that prices reflect that information.

Informed traders—buyers and sellers of securities with more information than others.

Inside traders—individuals trading while in possession of information relevant for making investment decision gained through a fiduciary relationship.

Insurance company—a firm that enters into contracts to bear risk of clients in return for premiums.

Keiretsu—a group of Japanese companies owning equity in each other and act in concert in their business operations.

Lender of last resort—the supplier of funds to banks and sometimes other types of financial institutions during times of liquidity crises. This role is typically performed by the central bank since it can create money and is never in danger of running out of domestic funds.

Making false statements—making any statement that is not true to a government official.

Market efficiency—the economic aspects of a securities market.

Market integrity—the aspects of a market dealing with the promulgation and enforcement of rules.

Market manipulation—trading in such a way as to create artificial prices or to deceive other traders.

Markets in Financial Instruments Directive (MiFID)—a European Union directive that is designed to harmonize and integrate regulation of financial markets within the Union.

Merit regulation—a regulator requires or prohibits certain actions.

Money laundering—disguising the illegal origin of funds.

Obstruction of justice—taking actions to hinder criminal investigations.

Painting the tape—buying and selling a security to create the illusion of active trading, attracting others to buy so that those operating the scheme can sell at a profit. Some also call this churning or wash trading.

Pareto efficiency—the status quo cannot be changed without making someone worse off.

Phishing—the fraudulent practice of sending emails disguised as being from reputable companies to induce the recipients to reveal personal data.

Ponzi scheme— a scheme to defraud investors by promising high returns and repaying early investors with money from later investors to give the appearance of successful operations.

Portfolio investment— the purchase of shares or debt securities as a passive investment.

Predatory lending—fraudulent, unfair, or deceptive practices in lending.

Premium—the payment received by an insurance company for bearing risk. (Note that there are a number of other definitions of this term in finance.)

Proprietary trading—a firm trading with its own funds for its own profit.

Prudent man rule—a U.S. rule that states that in making investments a trustee must act as others would act in making investments for themselves. The rule has been extended by ERISA to require that trustees act as others knowledgeable about making investments would act.

Regulation Fair Disclosure (Reg FD)—a regulation of the U.S. Securities and Exchange Commission that mandates the information be disclosed to professional investors and other investors at the same time.

Regulatory capture—the process whereby current and former industry members come to dominate the boards and staffs of regulatory bodies.

Run (banking)—the simultaneous withdrawal of deposits by the customers of a bank or other depositary institution.

Run (manipulation)—see painting the tape.

Sarbanes-Oxley Act (U.S.)—a law passed in 2002 to strengthen oversight of auditors and company financial statements.

Self-regulatory organizations—a organization with members that establish and enforce rules of conduct for securities firms.

Structuring—arranging financial transactions in such a way as to avoid filing requirements.

Systemic risk—risk that the failure of one counterparty to meet its obligations when due will result in the inability of other counterparties to meet their obligations when due, resulting in a collapse of the entire financial system. Also known as Herstatt risk.

Trust indenture—a formal agreement between the issuer of bonds and the bondholder.

Trustee (bankruptcy)—a court appointed individual who administers assets of a bankrupt individual or institution.

United Nations Convention against Corruption—an international treaty with more than 140 signatories that criminalizes basic forms of corruption such as bribery and embezzlement, trading in influence, money laundering, and obstruction of justice.

Universal banking—a system in which banks own or control a major portion of the shares in firms and participate actively in corporate governance.

Wash sale—see painting the tape.

IN THIS CHAPTER, we discuss how to raise new capital. Specifically, we:

- Explain three reasons for regulation, and
- Describe alternate approaches to regulation,

Then we review the scope of regulation dealing with

- Financial markets,
- Financial institutions,
- Nondomestic investors, and
- Multinational institutions.

We also address the relationship between market efficiency and market integrity and efforts to promote ethics and curb criminal activities.

1. Introduction

Comprehensive regulation of financial markets is relatively new and has grown substantially, especially since the 1930's when many banks collapsed and stock prices plummeted during the Great Depression, resulting in widespread losses by investors and savers. One goal of the regulations that have been adopted is to prevent the failure of one institution from spreading and causing the failure of the entire financial system. The continuing need for this type of regulation was made evident in 2008 when the collapse of the investment banking firm, Lehman Brothers, lead to a financial panic. The price of Wachovia Corp., the fourth largest bank holding company in the U.S. at the time, fell from more than 50 USD per share to about 1 USD per share and Wachovia was forced to sell itself to another bank, Wells Fargo.

Other goals of regulation are to protect consumers of financial products and investors, and to influence the financial system to help achieve societal objectives. Merit regulations require certain actions and prohibit others. Disclosure regulations attempt to provide investors with sufficient information to make informed decisions.

The Basel Committee develops common policies for the regulation of banks and the International Organization of Securities Commissions develops regulations for securities markets. As the world economy becomes more integrated, the coordination of regulation between countries is becoming more important. As a direct result of the financial crisis of 2008, the Basel Committee is completing a new standard for international bank regulation and reserve requirements, commonly referred to as Basel II. This regulatory effort is designed to improve transparency of the financial condition of banks by standardizing accounting and reporting practices.

2. Regulation

2.1. Reasons

2.1.1. Prevention of systemic risk

One reason for financial regulation is the presence of **systemic risk**, the risk that the problems of one firm or its failure will cause problems for other firms. Imprudent lending by one bank can cause it to fail, which, in turn, can cause depositors to lose faith in the banking system and to quickly withdraw their deposits from other institutions. Such a **run** could cause the collapse of the entire banking system. There were many bank runs in the

U.S. until the creation of government deposit insurance and the active efforts of the U.S. central bank, the Federal Reserve System, which can lend money to banks in distress.

Securities markets also have systemic risk. An initial decline in stock prices can lead to margin calls, which is a request for more margin or collateral. Inventors may be forced to sell stock to raise funds to meet the margin calls, further depressing prices and leading to further margin calls. This type of downward spiral can lead to the collapse of an investment banking firm's clients and to the collapse of the firm itself if its clients cannot meet their margin calls and end up owing the firm more than the value of their collateral. In the 1980s the Hunts, a wealthy Texas oil family, faced millions of USDs of margin calls on their derivative contracts. The U.S. Federal Reserve feared that failure to meet these margin calls would result in the bankruptcy of the brokerage firm holding their account, which, in turn, would precipitate a systemic crisis. To avert such a crisis the U.S. Federal Reserve arranged a loan for the family in exchange for asset pledges and also required that the family sell its silver holdings.

2.1.2. Protecting consumers and investors

Another important objective of regulation is to protect investors and the clients of financial institutions. Without regulation unscrupulous financial professionals may try to take advantage of unsophisticated investors. Indeed even with regulation investors still lose billions of USD to fraudsters each year. In one recent case Bernard Madoff took billions of USD from individuals and institutions ostensibly to invest the funds using sophisticated strategies. Instead, he spent much of the money on personal luxuries and used new clients' funds to repay older clients. The court-appointed trustee estimated losses to investors of 18 billion USD, not counting purported profits.

When the proportion of investors in a country grows the importance of investor protection also grows because generally the new investors are less sophisticated than the initial investors. Investors may need protection against insider trading and unfair use of corporate assets. The government may require all vendors of certain products to provide the same information in the same format so that consumers can compare these products and make more informed judgments. The government may bar financial institutions from discriminating against certain consumers on the basis of race or other characteristics.

2.1.3. Preventing predatory lending

Predatory lending occurs when unscrupulous actions are carried out by a lender to entice, induce and/or assist a borrower in taking a mortgage that carries high fees, a high interest rate, strips the borrower of equity, or places the borrower in a lower credit rated loan to the benefit of the lender. As with most things of a dishonest nature, new and different predatory lending schemes frequently arise.[1] An example of predatory lending is the so called 'liar loan', where a loan is granted to the borrower based on the borrower's stated income and assets without verification. Many of these loans were beyond the ability of the borrowers to repay.

2.1.4. Achieving societal objectives

Another reason for regulating financial markets and institutions is to promote societal objectives that are not feasible otherwise. The government may wish to support economic sectors such as housing. Since criminals typically use banks, the government may regulate financial institutions to prevent their use in the commission of crimes. In Malaysia the government favored the local Malay population by requiring that a certain proportion of new stock issues be set aside for them.

2.2. Alternate approaches

2.2.1. Self-regulation versus governmental regulation

Historically, financial markets have been largely self-regulated and a large measure of self-regulation continues. Self-regulation can have advantages over governmental regulation. Industry participants are likely to be more knowledgeable than governmental officials concerning the details of the operation of their businesses. Industry professionals also have self-interest in promoting fair dealing at least among themselves. Self-regulation can also

---

[1] Definition from http://www.investopedia.com/terms/p/predatory_lending.asp.

help to develop an ethical climate in which industry professionals go further than might be possible through government regulation. As Justice Douglas of the U.S. Supreme Court observed, self-regulation "has the potential for establishing and enforcing ethical standards beyond those that the law can establish."

Governmental regulation, on the other hand, may take broad-based societal issues (such as lowering transaction costs) into account more fully. Governments typically can impose more stringent penalties including large fines and prison sentences. In most cases the mere threat of criminal prosecution of a financial organization is sufficient to compel compliance. Governments may also have more resources to devote to regulation. A difficulty with governmental regulation is **regulatory capture** in which industry members, because of their more intense interest and greater expertise, co-opt the governmental regulatory process. Current and former industry members may come to dominate the boards and staffs of regulatory agencies causing them to promulgate regulations that favor the industry rather than its customers.

In the US, governmental regulation of the banking industry increased significantly with the creation of the U.S. Federal Reserve System in 1913. Debate as to the relative roles of self-regulation and governmental regulation is ongoing. Considering the role of regulation in establishing policies concerning banks' dealing in financial derivatives, Paul Volker, says:

> "Plainly, the authors believe that the amount of capital needed to support derivatives exposure is a matter of judgement for individual institutions, depending on their appetite for risk and their ability to measure and manage it…." (from the forward to the Group of Thirty's 1993 report).

Stock exchanges have always had rules. But until the worldwide market crash of 1929 there was little governmental regulation of securities markets. The crash prompted the U.S. to pass several pieces of legislation, including the Securities Act of 1933 and the Securities Exchange Act of 1934. In many cases this legislation continued to emphasize self-regulation, but within a statutory framework. The Securities and Exchange Commission is empowered to issue regulations governing the issuance and trading of securities and to enforce these regulations. But enforcement is also carried out through a number of **self-regulatory organizations** (SROs) including the stock exchanges themselves.[1]

The Consumer Financial Protection Bureau was established by the Dodd–Frank Wall Street Reform and Consumer Protection Act and began operations in 2011. The Bureau has broad jurisdiction over the financial services industry including banks, credit unions, securities firms, debt collectors, payday lenders, and various types of firms involved in mortgage lending and administration. The Bureau makes and enforces rules for these institutions. The Bureau is a unit within the U. S. Federal Reserve.

Rapid and substantial regulatory changes are taking place in the European Union in regard to market regulation. The EU has been attempting to create a single market for financial services. In 1999 Baron Alexandre Lamfalussy chaired a committee that developed a Financial Services Action Plan with 42 articles designed to harmonization the financial services markets. There were four directives: the Prospectus Directive, the Market Abuse Directive, the Transparency Directive and the **Markets in Financial Instruments Directive (MiFID)**. MiFID is fostering the implementation of rules to harmonize regulation of securities across the member states.[2] MiFID II is expected to be implemented by 2014.[3]

In January 2013, due to the failures of the financial regulators during the financial crisis beginning in 2008, the U.K. established a new regulatory structure. The Bank of England is the chief regulator. A Financial Policy Committee, the Prudential Regulation Authority and the Financial Conduct Authority were also established. These agencies have been given authority to go beyond mere auditing of financial services to establish "a regulatory culture of judgment, expertise and proactive supervision." The new regulations came into force on April 1, 2013.[4]

---

[1] The USSEC web site is: http://www.sec.gov/.

[2] http://blogs.law.harvard.edu/corpgov/2010/07/17/key-changes-to-the-eu-prospectus-directive/

[3] http://www.ft.com/cms/s/0/63351b14-1477-11e2-8cf2-00144feabdc0.html#axzz2MEPJWGmD

[4] http://www.hm-treasury.gov.uk/press_126_12.htm

2.2.2. Disclosure versus merit regulation

In **merit regulation** the government requires certain actions deemed to be in the public interest or prohibits certain actions that are deemed contrary to the public interest. The sale of specific financial products may be banned. The makeup of the board of directors may be specified. Specific securities may be reviewed and rejected for sale because they are too risky. Governments may also prohibit or require certain types of activities. In the U.S. the USSEC has prohibited stock exchanges from enforcing fixed commissions. Hence, each brokerage firm is free to set its own commission schedule and commissions are negotiable. Insider trading, price manipulation and other practices are typically prohibited.

Disclosure regulation focuses on ensuring that market participants fully disclose information so that investors can make knowledgeable decisions. In the U.S. the USSEC does not try to decide how much investors should pay for shares. Instead the SEC tries to make sure that companies disclose sufficient financial information to allow investors to make informed decisions. Detailed rules are provided concerning the nature of the information that must be disclosed and substantial penalties are imposed for violation of these rules. Disclosure is intended to prevent various types of problems, including conflicts of interest between a controlling owner and minority owners and between managers and owners. Sometimes controlling shareholders have sweetheart contracts with firms they are taking public in an IPO. These contracts may allow the controlling shareholder to charge above market rates for services rendered to the firm or to make purchases from the firm at below market rates. If investors buying shares in the IPO know in advance that a controlling shareholder has such a sweetheart contract, they can take this contract into account in valuing the firm. Hence, the value of the contracts to the controlling shareholder will be offset by a lower share price so that the controlling shareholder does not benefit at the expense of the new investors.

An example of discloser regulation is **Regulation Fair Disclosure** (Reg FD) adopted by the SEC in October 2003, which mandates that companies release information to the public and investment professionals at the same time. Prior to Reg FD, companies could disclose information concerning company performance to preferred firms or individuals. For example, if a company expected an increase in earnings, the company could disclose this information to a select group of investors or investment firms well before making the information publically available. Following the implementation of the regulation studies of earnings announcements report no change in return volatility, a significant increase in trading volume, and an increase in analyst forecast dispersion.[1] Another study shows a decline in the adverse selection component of the spread after the passage of the regulation, especially for smaller and thinner firms.[2] George Benston (1973) argues that disclosure rules are superfluous because markets will demand sufficient disclosure to insure fair pricing. If firms do not provide sufficient information, investors will refuse to buy the shares or will buy them only at a discount. This gives an incentive for those selling the share to provide more information. But if the selling shareholders are themselves minority shareholders without sufficient information, such as would likely be the case in a universal banking country described in the next section, they may not have any information to provide. In this type of market shares can sell at prices that vary significantly from their full-information price.

Bangladesh switched from merit regulation to disclosure regulation in 1999. However, lack of authority to regulate auditors and lawyers who are responsible for preparing prospectuses and lack of ability to sue on behalf of shareholders without shareholder class action diminished the effectiveness of disclosure regulation.

2.3. Alternate economic systems

The way in which an economy provides for risk sharing and corporate governance decision-making has an important influence on the regulation of its economic institutions. There are two primary economic mechanisms used to share risk and make corporate governance decisions in market economies—banks and stock markets.

---

[1] Bailey, Li, Mao, and Zhong (2003).

[2] Eleswarapu, Thompson, and Venkataraman (2004).

2.3.1. Universal banking

Universal banking is a system in which banks own or control a major portion of the shares in firms and participate actively in corporate governance. In addition to owning equity, banks are the primary underwriters of new equity offerings and also offer brokerage services.[1] In Germany banks often own both the debt and equity of a firm, which gives them a great deal of control over the firm. In addition, German banks typically have the right to vote the shares of others, such as trust accounts, that are left with the bank. Based on data for 1974, Gorton and Schmid (1996) report that large concentrated shareholdings by banks improved firm performance. And banks were special in that large holdings by other entities did not affect performance. But based on data for 1985 these authors no longer find that banks holdings affect firm performance. They attributed this decreased influence of banks to the fact that securities markets have become more developed, decreasing firms' reliance on banks. Kester (1994) also reports a positive role for banks, which can monitor management to help insure efficient operations, mediate disputes among stakeholders and even promote new business opportunities among related firms.

In Japan many companies are organized into groups called **keiretsu**. Keiretsu are characterized by cross holdings of equity among group members. In Japan perhaps two-thirds of corporate equity is held by other corporations. Since each keiretsu firm owns an interest in the other members of the group, control is vested in the current management rather than with the outside stockholders. The keiretsu may include a bank that functions as the main bank of most or all of the members of the group. The main bank often lends funds to group members and these loans are typically rolled over at maturity. Further, the main bank provides flexibility in that compensating balances and interest and principal payments can be deferred in times of adversity. Stockholders usually receive a fixed dividend payment that rarely changes and non-keiretsu stockholders usually have negligible influence on management.

---

[1] Van Hulle (1996) provides discussion and figures showing the ownership structures of a number of European holding groups.

In the main bank and universal bank system public information needs may be low since the banks can obtain information directly from the corporations in which they hold shares in the same way that they would when making loans to these corporations. Bank officials may be directors of the firms. Liquidity is less important because the banks are long term or even permanent investors in the enterprises in which they hold shares.

2.3.2. Stock markets

Stock markets allow investors to pool their funds, each buying shares according to their wealth and risk tolerance. The number of investors is relatively large and these investors typically select some or all of the governing boards of the firms in which they hold shares. Information must be disseminated widely and in a sufficiently simple form to permit understanding by numerous individuals.

2.4. Market quality

Regulators seek to promote market quality, which, as shown in Figure 5-1, has two aspects—market efficiency and market integrity. The International Organization of Securities Commissions recognizes both efficiency and fairness (i.e., market integrity) as goals of markets.[1]

Figure 5-1. Components of market quality

Market efficiency

- Transaction costs
- Price discovery

Market integrity

- Insider trading (trading ahead of price-sensitive announcements)
- Market manipulation (ramping, rumors)
- Broker-agency conflict (churning, front running)

Source: Figure 1, Aitken, Kwan, and McInish (2010).

---

1 http://www.law.harvard.edu/programs/about/pifs/symposia/europe/2010-europe/briefing-book/concept-papers/tanzer.pdf

Market efficiency, which is concerned with the economic aspects of a securities market, has received considerable attention. But regulators are also concerned with fairness. The U.K. regulator, the Financial Services Authority (FSA), states that an **efficient market** is "one in which users – at reasonable cost – can achieve optimum pricing for their type of transaction as a result of having adequate information on, and access to, current supply and demand, and in which participants have maximum choice of methods for minimizing their exposure to risk."[1]

Turning to **market integrity**, according to the FSA, "a **fair market** is one that is free of unfair practices and abuse, and in which all investors have reasonable opportunity to trade at the best price available for their transaction size."[2]

At least three broad categories of violations of market integrity are recognized, namely, informed trading, market manipulation, and broker/agency conflicts. We consider each of these, in turn, below beginning in section 2.4.2.

2.4.1. The tradeoff between efficiency and fairness

Shefrin and Statman (1993) examine financial market regulation in terms of two goals—efficiency and fairness. In some cases it may be possible to increase fairness without affecting efficiency or to increase efficiency without affecting fairness. In other cases this may not be possible so that there is a tradeoff between efficiency and fairness. Shefrin and Statman (1993) argue that policymakers operate as if there is an efficiency/fairness frontier exhibiting a maximum level of fairness for a given level of efficiency or a maximum level of efficiency for a given level of fairness. Movements along the frontier represent reduced fairness to gain increased efficiency or reduced efficiency to gain increased fairness. Of course, the efficiency/fairness frontier may be multidimensional in that there may also be tradeoffs among types of efficiency or categories of fairness.

These authors consider two types of efficiency. **Pareto efficiency** means that the *status quo* cannot be changed without making someone worse off. **Information efficiency** means that everyone has the same information and

---

1 http://www.fsa.gov.uk/pubs/discussion/d02.pdf

2 http://www.fsa.gov.uk/pubs/discussion/d02.pdf

a common analysis of that information so that prices reflect that information.

Shefrin and Statman (1993) identify seven dimensions of fairness, namely:

1. **Freedom from misrepresentation.** Securities issuers and financial professionals provide information that investors can rely upon. This is why the CFA Institute requires that its charter holders have a reasonable basis for their recommendations.
2. **Equal information.** It is typically considered unfair for some investors to have information that others do not have. This is the reason the U.S. Securities and Exchange Commission adopted Regulation Fair Disclosure, which requires firms to disseminate information to all investors at the same time.
3. **Equal information processing**. Individuals who are less sophisticated and have fewer analytical skills need to be protected. In a merit regulatory scheme certain types of transactions might be forbidden.
4. **Freedom from impulse.** Because it is know that some investors make cognitive errors and lack of self-control, certain transactions can be recanted for a limited time.
5. **Efficient prices.** Trading halts and restrictions on trading at prices outside of a range based on the previous trade price or the previous close might be used to protect investors from trading at unreasonable prices due to temporary supply-demand imbalances.
6. **Equal bargaining power.** Individuals who are not able to bargain effectively with institutions might be protected by maximum rates such as those provided in usury statues.

These dimensions of fairness may be conflicting. Protecting investors from their own impulses may reduce their freedom to take action.

2.4.2. Informed trading and illegal insider trading

Informed traders are privy to information that other market participants do not have. Some institutions spend a lot of money to collect information. For example, a commodities futures trading firm in Memphis, Tennessee, employees a meteorologists to forecast weather in South America, which provides valuable information about potential changes in the supply of crops that could influence their price. Brokerage firms employ analysts to study specific companies, regions and countries to forecast stock price movements. Observation of client order flow can also provide brokers with valuable information on the state of the market that can be useful in proprietary trading, which is the trading of brokers for their own profit.

Informed traders are more knowledgeable about a company than other traders. A subset of informed traders are **insider traders** engaging in **illegal insider trading**, which is trading on information by those with a fiduciary duty to the company such as officers, directors, and employees.

Trading by a company's lawyers and accounts and others with access to confidential information in the normal course of their dealings with the company may constitute illegal insider trading. Relatives of these individuals would also be included. However, someone who overheard a conversation at an adjoining table at lunch would not normally be legally barred from trading on that information. However, the Code of Ethics of the CFA Institute bars CFAs from trading on such information. Examining actual insider trading cases prosecuted by the Securities and Exchange Commission, McInish, Frino, and Sensenbrenner (2011) find that insiders trade strategically is a way that is consistent with trying to hide their trades. They trade more on high volume days. Overall, if they are selling they favor days on which the market is up. An exception is that insiders buy on days that have higher returns.

In October 2009 Raj Rajaratnam of the hedge fund Galleon Group and five others were charged with illegal insider trading by the SEC. The hedge fund managers were alleged to have traded on inside information about forthcoming earnings announcements.[1] Rajaratnam was found guilty in May 2011.

2.4.3. Market manipulation

Market manipulation is the act of creating an artificial price for a security. Portfolio managers may attempt to inflate the closing price to increase monthly gain and increase bonuses. Traders may try to inflate or deflate closing prices to affect option valuations. A typical example is that of SEC v. Kin Lee. In after hours trading Mr. Lee executed a number of trades that involved simultaneously buying and selling shares at gradually

---

[1] http://knowledge.wharton.upenn.edu/india/article.cfm?articleid=4422

higher prices to create the appearance of an active market with an increasing stock price. In the U.S. this type of trading is typically called **painting the tape**. Other terms that have more or less the same meaning include **wash sale**, **ramping**, **run** and **churning**. This false trading may induce other traders to enter the market as buyers pushing the price up so that the manipulator can sell at a profit. Market surveillance systems were able to detect Mr. Lee's actions even though he used multiple trading accounts from several brokerage houses to conduct his manipulative practices.[1]

In the 1980's four individuals paid 11 financial institutions 38 million USD to induce them to acquire shares of more than 300 million USD in Guinness stock. The financial institutions were indemnified against loss on their share purchases. Their goal was to artificially inflate Guinness' share price so that the firm could use these shares to acquire another firm. The individuals were charged with manipulating Guinness share prices. The heart of the case was that the indemnity unfairly advantaged the financial institutions. All four defendants were convicted in 1990.[2]

2.4.4. Broker-agency conflicts

Broker/agency conflicts represent another class of violations of market integrity. These violations of market integrity arise from a broker failing to honor its duty to its customers. **Frontrunning** is the illegal practice of a broker trading ahead of a client order to take advantage of the anticipated market impact of the client's trade. Buy side traders attempt to avoid being front run by engaging in practices such as splitting their orders among multiple brokers and trading through anonymous crossing networks. Another type of broker/client conflict is churning, excessive trading that benefits the broker by generating increased commissions without commensurate benefits for the client.

---

[1] Additional information on this event can be found at http://www.sec.gov/litigation/complaints/complr17579.htm.

[2] http://en.wikipedia.org/wiki/Guinness_share-trading_fraud

2.4.5. Best execution

In many countries the same security is traded in multiple markets, which may give rise to questions about how a brokerage firm should handle a client order if the markets differ on price or other characteristics such as available size or speed of execution. Most markets recognize a duty of **best execution**, which requires a broker to execute a trade in such a way that the client receives the best terms. But what constitutes best execution may not be straightforward. The problem with achieving best execution, as described in detail by Macey and O'Hara (1997), is that what is best for the client may depend on the tradeoff between multiple factors such as price and speed. Also, the understanding of what constitutes best execution often differs from jurisdiction to jurisdiction. In the U.S. brokers must consider multiple elements such as price, speed and size in determining best execution. However, in Japan brokerage firms are simply required to state how they will handle orders and to follow their stated policy.[1] Most brokerage firms in Japan send orders in securities traded in multiple markets to the market with the most historical volume in that security. Of course, such policies limit competition among exchanges.

2.4.6. Financial crimes

Ponzi schemes are named after Charles Ponzi who was the first widely know operator of such a scheme although he did not develop the fraud. Ponzi collected money from investors promising returns of 50% within 45 days and 100% within 90 days. He told these investors that he was using the money to buy discounted postal reply coupons outside the U.S. and redeeming them in the U.S., which is a form of arbitrage. In reality, he paid early investors with funds from later investors and also diverted some of the funds to his own use. Ponzi was convicted of mail fraud in 1922 and spent a number of years in jail. Ponzi schemes continue to be uncovered. In 2009 Bernard Madoff was convicted of crimes related to a Ponzi scheme

---

[1] For a typical example see: Diawa Capital Markets: In the case where the security [has] multiple listing, the order will be placed with the … exchange with the highest trading generated during a certain period. http://www.jp.daiwacm.com/english/execution.html

that operated over many decades and resulted in the loss of more the 18 billion USD. Madoff was sentenced to 150 years in prison. In 2012 Alan Stanford was convicted of operating a Ponzi scheme in connection with the sale of 7 billion USD of certificates of deposit in an off shore bank. Stanford was sentenced to 110 years in prison.[1]

Financial crimes include: corruption, kickbacks, fraud (**phishing**, stolen credit cards, identity theft, sick leave and overtime abuse, inventory theft, counterfeit checks, consumer fraud, collecting fees and not performing work, inflating financial results to earn bonuses, illegal price fixing, fraudulent activities by employees including embezzlement, mortgage fraud, click fraud, false travel and entertainment claims, ghost employees, ponzi scheme), theft (cash, intellectual property, identity theft, art theft), manipulation (bid rigging, inflated invoices, altering sales figures, diverting vendor discounts), computer-related crimes (software piracy, stealing personal data, attacks on the cyber infrastructure of an enterprise, maliciously entering others' computer systems), extortion, counterfeit currency, income tax crime, bankruptcy crime, and money laundering.

Fraudsters frequently use spam emails sent to thousands of individuals to tout stocks by making false or misleading statements to induce purchases. The promoters sending the emails sell their stock when this buying inflates the stock's price. To combat these emails, in 2003 the U.S. enacted a law called Controlling the Assault of Non-Solicited Pornography and Marketing (CAN-SPAM Act of 2003). One requirement of the act is that the email must indicate whether the sender is being compensated and if they are being compensated the nature of the compensation. A study of over 40,000 emails found that 60% provided the required disclosure. Spam emails showing the disclosure had a lower market impact, but still showed a decline in stock price from the peak of the spam campaign.[2]

Another study of stock span emails in the U.S. reports that abnormal return, turnover, and risk are significantly higher for spam e-mails containing a target price. Small investors react naively to spammers' forecasts. Further, if the spam e-mail mentioned that the firm was

---

[1] For additional examples of hedge fund fraud see Muhtaseb, Chun, and Yang (2008).

[2] Hu, McInish, Zeng (2009).

headquartered outside the U.S. or was doing business outside the U.S., U.S. recipients did not respond as much. Factors that did not affect recipients' response are e-mail length, e-mail source, and or whether the spammers received incentives.[1]

2.4.7. U.S. sentencing guidelines for corporations

The U.S. Sentencing Reform Act adopted in 1984 established the United States Sentencing Commission to promulgate uniform sentencing guidelines for the U.S. In 1991 the Commission developed Federal Sentencing Guidelines for Organizations that were approved by Congress. Under the Guidelines fines are determined by the offence level determined by the value of the commerce involved and the organization's culpability score, which are described in the Guidelines Manual.[2]

A base fine is established using the greatest of (1) an amount determined from a table, based on a fine derived from a table depending on the offense level, (2) the pecuniary gain to the organization from the offense; or (3) the pecuniary loss from the offense caused by the organization, to the extent the loss was caused intentionally, knowingly, or recklessly. Using a culpability score, the base level can be reduced up to 95% (for a score of 0 or less) or multiplied by 4 (for a score of 10 or more).

To determine the culpability score, begin with 5 points. Add points, depending on the size of the organization (up to five for very large organizations), if an individual within high-level personnel of the unit participated in, condoned, or was willfully ignorant of the offense. Add up to 2 points if the organization was convicted of similar misconduct within the last 10 years. Add up to 2 points if the misconduct violates a court order. Add 3 points if the organization obstructed justice. Subtract 3 points if the organization has an effective compliance and ethics program. Subtract up to 5 points based on whether the organization reported the misconduct prior to its discovery by outsiders and the extent to which the organization

---

[1] Hu, McInish, Zeng (2010).

[2] http://www.ussc.gov/Guidelines/Organizational_Guidelines/guidelines_chapter_8.htm

cooperated in the investigation and clearly demonstrated recognition and acceptance of responsibility.

The Guidelines provide for a possible reduction to the base fine if the organization has an effective compliance program. In 2004 the Guidelines were amended to make the requirements for an effective program more strict, and, in 2010, the Guidelines were amended to provide clearer guidance as to what constitutes an effective compliance program. To have an effective compliance and ethics program, an organization must (1) exercise due diligence to prevent and detect criminal conduct and (2) promote an organizational culture that encourages ethical conduct and a commitment to compliance with the law. At a minimum the organization must (1) establish standards and procedures to prevent and detect criminal conduct, (2) employ individuals in authority who are knowledgeable about ethics program and who provide reasonable oversight, and (3) communicate its standards regularly. After criminal conduct has been detected, the organization must report the conduct promptly to the appropriate governmental authorities and take steps to make sure the conduct is not repeated. The steps taken should include any modification needed in the organization's ethics and compliance program.

2.5. Bankruptcy

Bankruptcy, which is a legal process through which organizations restructure their finances, is an important type of regulation of financial activity. There are at least two important dimensions of bankruptcy law that differ from country to country. One is whether the goal of bankruptcy is to liquidate the firm or to promote the possibility that the firm will remain a going concern. A closely related issue concerns who controls an insolvent firm. In the UK, historically, about three-quarters of all reorganizations have been liquidations and about 22% have been receiverships. In liquidation a liquidator is appointed to sell enough of the firm's assets to repay creditors. The liquidator may sell the entire firm or parts of the firm, but the liquidation must proceed expeditiously. Alternately, a creditor with a type of claim known as a floating charge can unilaterally appoint a receiver for the firm. The appointment of a receiver typically does not require the permission of a court. When a receiver is appointed, control of the firm passes to the receiver and the board of directors steps down. The goal of the receiver is to liquidate the firm for the benefit of the appointing creditor and the receiver has little or no duty of care to other stakeholders, including stockholders, employees, the government, and other creditors. The receivership law does not provide for an **automatic stay** in which other creditors are prevented from pursuing their claims in court. The ability of the receiver to operate the firm as a going concern pending liquidation may be hampered by the fact that creditors with claims against specific assets, called fixed charges, can reposes those assets even if they are vital to the operation of the business.

In contrast to the UK, in the U.S. debtors usually have a much more important role in cases of corporate insolvency. There are two main bankruptcy provisions—Chapter 7 and Chapter 11. Under Chapter 7 the court appoints a trustee to oversee the liquidation of the firm. The firm is closed down and the assets are sold under the supervision of the trustee. Under Chapter 11 the directors of the firm remain in control of the firm, which continues to operate. This is referred to as **debtor-in-possession**. In about one-half of the cases the existing management remains in control and in most of the other cases new management is appointed. The filling of a bankruptcy petition causes an automatic stay, i.e., a suspension of any actions that creditors might take to enforce their claims. Further, those who have supplied equipment and buildings to the firm through leases are not likely to be able to reclaim their property until the reorganization plan is approved.

The **absolute priority rule** states that each senior class of creditors receives full payment before any junior class or equity holders receive any payments. The absolute priority rule is not a part of U.S. bankruptcy law and deviations are common.[1] A creditors committee is appointed to negotiate with management, who for an initial period, retain the exclusive right to present a plan to the court. The creditors committee has representatives of each impaired class, those receiving less than their contractual obligation. To be approved a plan must receive the assent of each impaired class by majority vote in terms of numbers and by a two-

---

[1] Beranek, Boehmer and Smith (1996). For a more theoretical discussion of the absolute priority rule see Longhofer (1977),

thirds vote in terms of USD value of claims. If one or more impaired classes reject the plan, it fails. If all impaired classes reject the plan the negotiations must continue or the firm must be liquidated. If one impaired class accepts the plan the court may still order implementation of the plan which is forced on the dissenting creditors. This is called a **cramdown.** Box 5-1 reviews the mother of all cramdowns for one of the largest bankruptcies in U.S. history; the failure of General Motors.

Box 5-1: The GM bankruptcy

On June 1, 2009, a weak economy, reduced auto sales, large debt and pension obligations, and a very weak credit market led General Motors to filed for Chapter 11 bankruptcy protection. GM had 172.81 billion USD in debt, making this the largest bankruptcy of a non-financial firm in U.S. history. Assets totaled 82.29 billion USD. In an attempt to avoid bankruptcy, GM offered senior debt holders 225 shares of GM stock for every $1,000 of debt held, or roughly 10 cents on the dollar. Believing that existing bankruptcy law and precedent was on their side, bond holders held out for a better deal and continued negotiations with GM, the UAW, and the U.S. government. However, ultimately, the bond holders were not able to withstand the pressure. In the final settlement the U.S. government received an ownership stake of 60%, the Canadian government, 12.5%, the UAW, 17.5% and the bond holders 10%. Secured bond holders received 25 cents on the dollar, but the UAW was able to negotiate a settlement of 75 cents on the dollar of its unsecured obligations.

Source:
http://www.pittsburghlive.com/x/pittsburghtrib/business/s_629973.html

Bankruptcy law affects the operations of both solvent and insolvent firms. The effect on insolvent firms may be obvious. But the financing arrangements, investment decisions and other aspects of the operations of solvent firms may be affected by bankruptcy practices that will become applicable if the firm becomes insolvent. Creditors and equity investors must factor bankruptcy laws into their projections when they enter into investments.

Franks, Nyborg, and Torous (1996) propose three criteria for judging the efficiency of a bankruptcy code:

Does it preserve promising enterprises while liquidating uneconomic ones?

Does it allow the firm to be reorganized or liquidated at minimum cost?

Does it permit innovations in debt contracts to improve the insolvency process?

Another question that might be added to this list is: Does it treat non-equity and non-creditor stakeholders such as employees, customers, and governments fairly?

Many countries, especially those with relatively young capital markets, do not have well-developed bankruptcy laws. Lack of these laws can be detrimental. Enterprises that are inefficient may be able to continue operating even when they are insolvent because they cannot be forced to liquidate if their debts are not paid. In many countries that have written laws governing bankruptcy, however, due to bribery, favoritism, and other forms of corruption, bankruptcy laws are not equitably enforced. It is not the mere presence of bankruptcy laws that provide protection and economic stability, but a history of equitable enforcement is also required to make these laws useful.

2.6. Regulation of U.S. markets

We are interested in describing the various sorts of regulation faced by financial markets and financial institutions. Because the U.S. has a relatively comprehensive set of regulatory organizations, we briefly describe these. Later in this chapter we describe the regulation of U.S. financial institutions. Similar financial services and regulatory needs are found around the world.

Some of the first regulations for financial markets in the U.S. concerned the appropriate behavior of trustees who invested money for others. Traditionally, in English law trustees were limited in their investments to an English Court of Chancery list of government securities. In the U.S. a case was brought against the trustees of a trust established for the benefit of Harvard College. The trust document had directed the trustees to "loan the same upon ample and sufficient security, or to invest the same in sage and productive stock, either in the public funds, bank shares of other stock, according to their best judgment and discretion...." The trustees invested in several banks and insurance companies and in two manufacturing companies. Two trust remainder men sued the trustees seeking to recover the decline in value of the insurance and manufacturing stocks as not suitable trust investments. In 1830 in Harvard College v. Amory the court rejected the English rule saying that the available U.S. government securities were "exceedingly limited compared with the amount of trust funds to be invested" throughout the US. Further, since mortgages, real estate and all types of investments fluctuate in value, the judge concluded that "Do what you will, the capital is at hazard." The judge then announced what has come to be known as the prudent man rule, namely:

> All that can be required of a trustee to invest, is, that he shall conduce himself faithfully and exercise a sound discretion. He is to observe how men of prudence, discretion and intelligence manage their own affairs, not in regard to speculation, but in regard to the permanent disposition of their funds, considering the probably income, as well as the probable safety of the capital invested.

The prudent man rule was not widely adopted in the U.S. at first. Instead, state legislatures adopted legal lists of securities that were suitable for trust investments. These legal lists typically included only U.S. government and high-quality corporate bonds and common stocks were not permitted. These legal lists restricted most trust investments in the U.S. until the 1940s. With the collapse in bond values and the bankruptcy of many established firms in the Great Depression of the 1930s dissatisfaction with the legal list approach grew and the prudent man rule came to predominate. The prudent man rule is still influential. In the U.S. pension plans are regulated by the Department of Labor, which enforces the Employee Retirement Income Security Act of 1974 (ERISA). ERISA requires that those running pension plans act with the "care, skill, prudence, and diligence" of those who are knowledgeable in their field and requires that the plan be managed for the exclusive benefit of the beneficiaries.

Prior to 1911 securities markets in the U.S. were not regulated by either the federal or state governments. J.N. Dolly, the Banking Commissioner for the State of Kansas, begin a trend toward state regulation. Dolly believed that regulation was needed to prevent individuals from being lured into unprofitable investments by unscrupulous investment bankers. Legislation was passed requiring the approval of the Banking Commissioner before any security could be sold in the state. After the passage of the Kansas legislation similar laws were passed in most other U.S. states. These state laws regulating the sale of securities are called **blue sky laws**. Some states simply mandated better disclosure, but most attempted to assess the merits of issues before granting approval. While the protection of investors was the stated motive for this legislation, Macey and Miller (1991) argue that the real motive was to protect banks, which offered relatively low interest rates, from competition and higher-yielding securities. State bank regulators, small bankers, farmers and small businessmen supported the push for regulation. The farmers and small businessmen were interested in ensuring the availability of credit and in keeping its cost low. Large banks, investment bankers and large issuers of securities opposed the legislation. Eventually many securities issues such as those listed on stock exchanges were exempted from regulation in most states. Beginning in 1933 the U.S. government began to regulate securities markets, but state regulation continued in tandem with federal regulation.[1]

In the early 21st century the U.S. has a variety of U.S. government entities regulating financial markets and institutions. The U.S. Securities and Exchange Commission (USSEC) has the responsibility for enforcing many U.S. securities laws. The Securities Exchange Act of 1934 requires disclosure of information concerning securities, especially those traded publicly on exchanges or over-the-counter, outlaws fraudulent practices such as insider trading, and establishes regulations for market participants including margin rules.

The Securities Act (of 1933) requires the dissemination of information about securities that is relevant to making decisions concerning these securities and prohibits fraud in the sale of financial instruments. The Investment Company Act of 1940 provides for the regulation of investment companies. The Investment Adviser Act of 1940 requires that individuals or firms that are compensated for advising others about securities investment register and conform to standards promulgated under the Act. Under the Public Utility Holding Company Act of 1935 holding companies involved

---

[1] A directory of state securities regulators is provided at: http://www.sec.gov/consumer/state.htm.

in the electric utility business or in the retail distribution of natural or manufactured gas are subject to regulation. The Trust Indenture Act of 1939 requires that in addition to being registered with the USSEC all debt securities offered for public sale must have a **trust indenture**, a formal agreement between the issuer of bonds and the bondholder that conforms to the requirements of the Act.

In 2002 the U.S. adopted the **Sarbanes-Oxley Act** (SOX) formally known as "An Act to protect investors by improving the accuracy and reliability of corporate disclosures made pursuant to the securities laws, and for other purposes." The Act strengthens oversight of auditors by establishing a Public Company Accounting Oversight Board, providing for the independence of auditors, and making a company's senior officers responsible for the truthfulness of the firm's financial statements. The Act requires that the Chief Executive Officer sign the firm's tax returns. The Act establishes rules for financial analysts and provides penalties for the destruction of financial records and interfering with investigations, and provides protections for whistleblowers.

Other U.S. government entities with substantial regulatory authority over financial institutions include the Federal Deposit Insurance Corporation, the Federal Reserve, and the Office of the Comptroller of the Currency, and the Office of Thrift Supervision, and the National Credit Union Administration. A credit union is a financial institution created and owned by its members who are the only ones allowed to use its services. Two bureaus of the Department of the Treasury are active in the regulation of U.S. banks. The Office of the Comptroller of the Currency charters and regulates national banks. The Office of Thrift Supervision regulates other thrift institutions to maintain their safety and soundness. In the U.S. derivatives markets are regulated by the Commodity Futures Trading Commission. The CFTC reviews new contracts and conducts market surveillance. The Employee Retirement Income Security Act of 1974 (ERISA) is a U.S. law that sets minimum standards for most voluntarily established private pension and health plans. The law establishes fiduciary obligations for the managers of these plans and provides that the funds in the plan must be used for the exclusive benefit of the plan members.[1]

---

[1] http://www.dol.gov/dol/topic/health-plans/erisa.htm

Savings and Loan Associations (S&Ls) are financial institutions whose primary mission historically was the provision of credit for housing, but the removal of restrictions on the types of investments S&Ls can hold has made it increasingly difficult to distinguish them from banks. In 1989 regulation of S&Ls was given to the Department of the Treasury's Office of Thrift Supervision. As a result of the financial crisis of 2008 the U.S. enacted the Dodd-Frank Wall Street Reform and Consumer Protection Act. The act creates new U.S. government agencies to regulate financial markets, including the Financial Stability Oversight Council, the Office of Financial Research, and the Bureau of Consumer Financial Protection. Insurance companies are regulated by individual states. The National Association of Insurance Commissioners develops model laws and regulations concerning insurance regulation, which it recommends to the states.

A number of self-regulatory organizations (SROs) also have an obligation to monitor the financial markets. Each stock exchange is a SRO. The **Financial Industry Regulatory Authority** (FINRA), which is the successor to the **National Association of Securities Dealers,** is a private organization with authority to regulate the conduct of member brokerage firms and exchanges.

One function performed by SROs and others is market surveillance, the monitoring of order flow to ensure that market rules are followed. An example of regulatory-type activities of an exchange is the Stock Watch of the NYSE, which is a computerized system for monitoring unusual trading activity to help prevent price manipulation and insider trading. These automated monitoring systems are quite sophisticated and have lead to a number of cases for stock price manipulation. In 2010 NASDAQ acquired Smarts Group, an Australia-based market surveillance business that helps exchanges monitor compliance with trading rules. Smarts Group clients include more than 30 exchanges and regulators.

2.7. Regulation of non-U.S. markets

Many governments discriminate against non-citizens and restrict either portfolio investment, direct investment, or both. **Portfolio investments** refer to purchases of shares (or bonds) as a passive investment. As an example of portfolio investment restrictions, Qantas, an Australian airline, is subject to an aggregate foreign ownership limit of 49%. **Direct investment** in which companies buy existing businesses or establish new businesses may also be limited. Nondomestic firms may only be permitted to own minority interests in local firms. Local branches of nondomestic banks may not be permitted to participate fully in the local banking market. Both deposit seeking and lending may be restricted. Entry restrictions are common in financial services for most developing countries and even for a few developed countries. Canada, Finland, Iceland, Norway and Japan either currently restrict or have recently restricted ownership of companies. Participation in industries that are considered essential for the national defense are often restricted or prohibited. Rupert Murdoch, an Australian and founder of Newscorp, became a U.S. citizen to avoid U.S. limits on ownership of U.S. television stations.

2.8. Multinational regulation

2.8.1. Basel Committee

In 1974, after the collapse of the Herstatt Bank in Germany, the Group of Ten plus Switzerland and Luxembourg established the Standing Committee on Banking Regulations and Supervisory Practices known as the Basel Committee. Unlike central bankers, bank supervisory officials had previously been domestically focused. The Basel Committee provided these officials with an opportunity to meet, most for the first time. The Basel Committee on banking supervision focuses on two aspects of bank regulation —supervision and rules for internationally active banks.

In 1975 the Basel Committee reached an agreement embodying the idea that the basic aim of international regulation is to insure that no bank escapes supervision. Moreover, the Committee adopted the principle that banks' international business should be monitored on a consolidated basis and that primary responsibility is allocated to the home country of the parent. In 1988 the Committee proposed rules subsequently implemented by EU members. Under these rules banks were required to maintain shareholders' capital equal to 4% of risk-weighted assets (including off balance sheet activities) and to maintain a total capital ratio of 8% of an expanded list of assets and liabilities, including items such as loan loss reserves and subordinated debt. The Committee has also helped to make the disclosure of financial information more uniform and to modify secrecy laws so that information needed to insure adequate regulation of international banks can be exchanged.

The Basel Committee continues to work on strengthening the international regulatory environment for banks. Initially published in 2004, a framework called Basel II is founded on three pillars of regulatory focus. The first pillar focuses on the calculation of minimum capital reserves. Under Basel II these calculations must consider credit risk, market risk, and the operational risk. Overall Basel II will require banks to hold larger liquid reserves, decreasing risk, but also decreasing potential economic growth. The second pillar is meant to identify risk factors not captured in pillar 1, giving regulators discretion to adjust the regulatory capital requirements against that calculated under the first pillar. Pillar 3 is designed to increase the transparency of lenders' risk profile by requiring them to give details of their risk management and risk distributions. Information is released through the normal mandatory financial statements lenders are required to publish or through lenders' websites.[1] Basel II was superseded by Basel III prior to implementation and Basel III has not been implemented as of late 2013.

2.8.2. International Organization of Securities Commissions (IOSCO)

The International Organization of Securities Commissions was established in 1974 by securities and futures regulators by countries within the Americas and was expanded in 1983 to include regulators in all major developed and emerging markets.[2] The General Secretariat of IOSCO is in Montreal. Entities joining IOSCO must agree:

- to cooperate together to promote high standards of regulation in order to maintain just, efficient and sound markets,
- to exchange information on their respective experiences in order to promote the development of domestic markets,

---

[1] http://www.cml.org.uk/cml/policy/issues/748

[2] The IOSCO web address is: http://www.iosco.org/iosco.html.

- to unite their efforts to establish standards and an effective surveillance of international securities transactions, and
- to provide mutual assistance to promote the integrity of the markets by a rigorous application of the standards and by effective enforcement against offenses.

The objectives and principles of securities regulations as set forth by the International Organization of Securities Commissions (IOSCO) are to protect investors, ensure that markets are fair, efficient and transparent; and to reduce systemic risk. IOSCO sets out 30 principles of securities regulation that are grouped into eight categories.[1]

IOSCO has four regional committees that discuss regional problems, namely: Africa / Middle East, Asia/Pacific, European, and Inter-American. In addition there are two important standing committees. The Technical Committee reviews issues related to securities and derivative transactions and co-ordinates the response of members. The Technical Committee deals with: multinational disclosure and accounting, regulation of secondary markets, regulation of market intermediaries, enforcement and the exchange of information, investment management, and credit rating agencies.

The Emerging Markets Committee's goal is to promote developing securities and derivatives markets by establishing standards and training programs and by promoting the exchange of information. Topics addressed by the committee include:

Disclosure and accounting,
Regulation of secondary markets,
Regulation of market intermediaries,
Enforcement and the exchange of information and
Investment management.

2.8.3. Other international efforts

There are also a number of ongoing international efforts that affect international securities markets and the ethical behavior of individuals who participate in these markets. The Organization for Economic Cooperation

---

[1] International Organization of Securities Commissions. Objectives and Principles of Securities Regulation. June 2010. http://www.financialstabilityboard.org/cos/cos_100601.htm

and Development (OECD) is an organization comprising 29 members who meet to develop and improve economic and social policy.`[1] On 21 November 1997, OECD member countries and five non-member countries adopted a Convention on Combating Bribery of Foreign Public Officials in International Business Transactions. [2] This Convention deals with the offence committed by the person who promises or gives the bribe, in contrast with the person receiving the bribe. The convention permits signatories to co-ordinate efforts to combat bribery of public officials.

Money laundering, the processing of criminal funds in order to disguise their illegal origin, is a crime in many countries. The United Nations Office on Drugs and Crime estimates that in 2009 criminal activity represented 3.6 % of global gross domestic product and that 2.7% of gross domestic product was laundered.[3] In 1970 the U.S. enacted the Bank Secrecy Act to fight money laundering. To combat money laundering the U.S. Bank Secrecy Act mandates that businesses keep records and file reports designed to facilitate criminal activity including terrorism and tax evasion.[4]

Regulators have recently turned their attention to artificial currencies that are created by private entities. These currencies allow the transfer of funds anonymously. Regulators are concerned that these artificial currencies may be used to launder money. The most prominent artificial currency is bitcoin.[5] There are also other payment networks that are outside the banking system. **Hawala networks** involve a large number of money brokers who are able to transfer money for clients. This networks operate primarily in the Middle East, India, and Africa.[6]

Causing or attempting to cause a bank to fail to file a required report is the crime of **structuring.**[7] Structuring may involve keeping deposits at a

---

[1] Additional information on the convention can be found at the OECD web site: http://www.oecd.org/. This site provides.

[2] These were: Argentina, Brazil, Bulgaria, Chile and the Slovak Republic.

[3] http://www.fatf-gafi.org/pages/faq/moneylaundering/

[4] http://www.irs.gov/Businesses/Small-Businesses-&-Self-Employed/Bank-Secrecy-Act

[5] http://en.wikipedia.org/wiki/Bitcoin

[6] http://en.wikipedia.org/wiki/Hawala

[7] http://www.ffiec.gov/bsa_aml_infobase/pages_manual/olm_107.htm

given bank over multiple days under a reporting limit such as 10,000 USD or the depositing of sums lower than the reporting requirement at multiple banks possibly on a number of days.

Here is an example:

> "John Smith sells a car and goes to the bank with $14,000 in cash to deposit. He fills out a deposit slip and goes to the teller. As she starts to process the transaction, she states she needs his identification so she can fill out a currency transaction report. Well he is in no mood to let anyone "know his business," so he asks if he deposits $9,000 will a report need to be filled. The teller tells him that no report would be filled for a $9,000 deposit. So he takes $5,000 back and deposits just $9,000 on that day. Even if he never deposits the remaining $5,000, he altered the original deposit (the taking back of $5,000) and is guilty of structuring."[1]

In 1988, the United Nations adopted the Convention Against Illicit Traffic in Narcotic Drugs and Psychotropic Substances (the Vienna Convention). The Vienna Convention obliges signatories to make money laundering a crime and also requires them to facilitate the identification, tracing, seizure, and forfeiture of the proceeds of narcotics trafficking and money laundering. The United Nations operates the International Money Laundering Information Network, an Internet-based network that assists governments in fighting money laundering.[2]

Since criminals typically use the banking system to transact some of their business, governments have imposed regulations on money laundering in an effort to hinder illegal activities. In the US, banks are required to report currency transactions of 10,000 USD or more. Switzerland eliminated anonymous bank accounts in 1992 so that it could better police illegal activities

The Financial Action Task Force on Money Laundering[3] (FATF) was established as an inter-governmental body by the G-7 Summit in Paris in

---

[1] http://amlassassin.wordpress.com/2010/01/13/structuring-and-smurfing/

[2] For more information about these efforts see: https://www.imolin.org/.

[3] The organization's web address is: http://www.fatf-gafi.org/pages/0,2987,en_32250379_32235720_1_1_1_1_1,00.html .

1989 to examine measures to combat money laundering. In April 1990, the FATF issued forty recommendations designed to provide a comprehensive blueprint for action against money laundering. These recommendations were modified in 1996. The goal is to prevent the use of these funds to facilitate further criminal activity and to prevent the funds from being used to affect legitimated commerce.

A recent focus of money laundering regulation has been the funding of international terrorism. The Patriot Act amended the Bank Secrecy Act and was adopted after the 9/11 attacks. The goal of these amendments was to prevent, detect, and prosecute those people and organizations used to fund terrorist activities.

3. Ethics

3.1. The need for ethical behavior

Finance professionals deal with other people's money. Hence, they are often faced with temptation. There are opportunities to take advantage of clients, increasing one's own income and wealth at the client's expense. Further, the fact that the sums involved are typically large makes the temptation greater. These factors heighten the importance of integrity and ethics as an integral part of the finance profession.[1]

Financial professionals may engage in many types of unethical behavior. Besides frontrunning, churning, and insider trading described above, ethical lapses may include failure to disclose conflicts of interest, favoring some clients over others without a proper basis, plagiarizing the work of others, making recommendations that are unsuitable for the client, and trading on or communicating inside information. Unethical behavior can seriously damage this reputational capital, reducing income and profits. Hence, there is an incentive for the finance profession to promote ethical behavior by its practitioners.

In August 1991 Solomon Brothers, a major U.S. investment banking firm, disclosed that it had made illegal bids on U.S. government securities. As a

---

[1] In 1980 the USSEC required all fund companies to have an ethical statement. The code of ethics of Fidelity Investments can be found at: http://www451.fidelity.com:80/about/world/ethics_code.html.

result of these activities the firm was forced to pay fines of 122 million USD to the U.S. Treasury, 68 million USD to the U.S. Justice Department and to establish an indemnity fund of 100 million USD to pay claims from civil lawsuits arising out of the scandal, with any undistributed amount going to the U.S. Treasury. But the cost of the scandal is more fully captured by the fall in Solomon's stock value during the week the scandal was announced by about 1.5 billion USDs (see Box 5-3 for additional details). The value of firm reputation is underscored by the findings that underwriters who are subject to USSEC investigations "experience large declines in IPO market share" and the "stock prices of their clients decline significantly." [1]

In 1996 Daiwa Bank was sentenced to pay a fine of 340 million USD for conspiring to conceal trading losses of 1.1 billion USD from the U.S. government.[2] The bank's top management learned of the losses in July 1995 and confirmed them through its own investigation in early August, but refrained from reporting them until the end of September so that they could be reported along with the bank's regularly-scheduled financial statements. The Japanese Ministry of Finance had advised the bank that the report could have significant negative impact on Japanese financial markets. In the time between their discovery and reporting the bank knowingly filed a number of false forms to conceal the losses. According to U.S. sentencing guidelines for corporations, corporations can be held accountable for the transgressions of their employees. Firms that have made sincere and effective efforts to eliminate criminal activity may receive reduced penalties if the court believes that violations occurred despite their best efforts. The U.S. attorney in the case told the court:

It is virtually impossible for any financial institution to protect itself against every potential criminal act by its employees, particularly given the highly specialized nature and complexity of the securities now traded in the world's capital markets. It is precisely because of this complexity, however, that it is essential that corporations institute and insist upon a corporate

---

1 Beatty, Bunsis, and Hand (1998).

2 For additional information about this case see LeClair, Ferrell, and Fraedrich (1998).

Box 5-3: The Solomon Case

The U.S. Treasury regularly conducts auctions in which bonds are sold to the highest bidder, the next highest bidder, and so forth. When a price is reached that exhausts the available supply each bidder at that price receives an allocation equal to the ratio of their quantity sought to the total quantity sought at that price.

In the four-year U.S. Treasury note auction for June 1990 Solomon Brothers submitted a bid for bonds with a face value of more than 100% of the bonds being sold. In an auction of U.S. government agency bonds in July 1990, Solomon Brothers again submitted a bid for bonds with a face value greater than was being offered. The U.S. Treasury rejected this bid and limited bids to 35% of the bonds being offered.

Beginning in December 1990 Solomon submitted bids for 35% of the bonds available in nine auctions. In each of these auctions Solomon also submitted bids for a significant percentage of the bonds being offered in the name of a client. These client bids were unauthorized. In April 1991 the U.S. Treasury sent a warning letter to the client.

After learning of the warning letter, the person responsible for the bids, Paul Mozer, informed Solomon's Chairman, President, and General Counsel that he has made bids that violated Treasury regulations. These individuals took no immediate action.

In June 1991, after receiving a subpoenas from the U.S. Securities and Exchange Commission, Solomon initiated a review of the bidding and issued a press release.

In August 1991, the U.S. Treasury prohibited Solomon from bidding for customer accounts. The Federal Reserve Bank of New York suspended trading with Solomon for two months. Solomon created reserves for a potential loss of 385 million USD in fines and penalties. Numerous clients suspended trading with Solomon. The Chairman, President, and General Counsel resigned and Mr. Mozer was suspended.

Based on Smith, Clifford W., Jr., Economics and Ethics: The case of Salomon Brothers, Financial Management Collection 7, 3-7.

culture of absolute compliance with the rules and regulations of the marketplace. One of the most important ways to do this is to establish and enforce a system of internal controls and checks and balances that are designed to protect against the criminal acts of corporate employees.

3.2. Efforts to fight corruption and foster ethics

3.2.1. Governmental efforts

The **United Nations Convention against Corruption** became effective on 14 December 2005. The Convention established model policies to prevent both private and public corruption. The Convention criminalizes basic forms of corruption such as bribery and embezzlement, money laundering, and obstruction of justice. **Obstruction of justice** is the taking officials or witnesses or destroying or encouraging others to destroy evidence is obstruction of justice. Countries pledged to help in the recovery of plundered wealth. The Convention has more than 140 signatories.[1]

In 1995, the Independent Commission Against Corruption established the Hong Kong Ethics Development Centre comprising members from leading chambers of commerce in Hong Kong. More than 1,000 companies have used the resources of the Centre.[2]

In the U.S. a crime (a violation of U.S. Code 1001) commonly known as "making false statements" involves a person or organization that:

"knowingly and willfully-

(1) falsifies, conceals, or covers up by any trick, scheme, or device a material fact;

(2) makes any materially false, fictitious, or fraudulent statement or representation; or

---

[1]http://www.unodc.org/unodc/en/treaties/CAC/convention-highlights.html#Criminalization

[2] Additional information can be found at the following web addresses: Independent Commission Against Corruption,
http://www.cuhk.edu.hk/icac/index.htm;
The Hong Kong Ethics Development Centre,
http://www.cuhk.edu.hk/icac/edc.htm.

(3) makes or uses any false writing or document knowing the same to contain any materially false, fictitious, or fraudulent statement or entry; shall be fined under this title, imprisoned not more than 5 years or, if the offense involves international or domestic terrorism (as defined in section 2331), imprisoned not more than 8 years, or both."[1] of an act designed to hinder a criminal investigation.

In 2004 a well-known entrepreneur and television personality, Martha Stewart, was investigated for insider trading. She was never actually charged with insider trading, but was nevertheless convicted of making false statements and obstruction of justice in connection with the insider trading investigation.[2].

The U.S. **Foreign Corrupt Practices Act** makes it unlawful for a U.S. person to make a payment to a non-U.S. official to obtain business. The act also applies to non-U.S. persons while in the U.S. Foreign officials include anyone working directly or indirectly (say through a state owned enterprise) for a foreign government. The amount of any money or gift offered is not a consideration. Many companies employ firms to monitor their compliance and help identify government officials subject to the act. However, some types of payments, including "grease payments," may be permissible under the act. Grease payments are made to officials to obtain expedited performance of duties that they are already required to perform.

3.2.2. Private efforts to fight corruption

The CFA Institute is a global, nonprofit organization of investment professionals. The Institute awards the designation Chartered Financial Analyst (C.F.A.), the most widely recognized and prestigious professional certification in finance. The C.F.A. is awarded after the candidate passes a series of three examinations. The program takes a minimum of two and one-half years to complete. Major subject areas covered in these examinations include economics, accounting, finance, portfolio management, and ethics. As of November 2010 there were about 84,500 charter holders in 133 countries and 65,000 candidates in 154 countries.

1

http://stromlawfederaldefense.com/1001-violations-false-statements/

2 http://en.wikipedia.org/wiki/Martha_Stewart

The CFA Institute has a written Code of Ethics to which its members must adhere. Ethical analysts must both "act with integrity" and "maintain and improve their professional competence." This Code and the related Standards of Professional Conduct enumerate the fundamental responsibilities of a financial analyst and the minimum requirements that must be observed in the analyst's relationships with others in the profession, employers, clients and prospective clients, and the investing public. The Code and Standards apply to members worldwide. The first standard requires that members "comply with all applicable laws, rules, and regulations … of any government, regulatory organization, licensing agency, or professional association governing their professional activities. In the event of conflict, Members and Candidates must comply with the more strict law, rule, or regulation. [1]

Transparency International is a Berlin-based organization with chapters in fifteen countries that fight official corruption by promoting and strengthening international and national integrity. According to Transparency International: "Corruption is one of the greatest challenges of the contemporary world. It undermines good government, fundamentally distorts public policy, leads to the misallocation of resources, harms the private sector and private sector development and particularly hurts the poor. Controlling it is only possible with the cooperation of a wide range of stakeholders in the integrity system, including most importantly the state, civil society, and the private sector. There is also a crucial role to be played by international institutions." This organization also conducts an annual survey regarding the perception of corruption for each country and publishes the results [2]

4. Summary

Historically, financial markets have been largely self-regulated and this practice continues through self-regulatory organizations such as stock exchanges. Government regulation of financial markets increased

[1] The AIMR Code of Ethics is available at:
http://www.cfapubs.org/doi/pdf/10.2469/ccb.v2010.n14.1

[2] http://www.transparency.org/

substantially during the first half of the twentieth century. Governments seek to prevent systemic risk, protect consumers of financial products, and achieve social objectives. Systemic risk occurs when the failure of one participant in the financial markets causes the failure of other participants, potentially leading to the collapse of the entire financial system.

Two alternate forms of regulation are merit regulation and disclosure regulation. Under merit regulation governments prohibit or require certain types of activities or pass judgment on the suitability of certain investments. Under disclosure regulation the government focuses on ensuring that market participants fully disclose information so that investors can make knowledgeable decisions. Governments regulate the activities of financial markets and financial institutions and the access of nondomestic investors to domestic markets.

The types of regulations needed may depend on the particulars of the financial system in a given country. If the primary mechanism for risk sharing is through banking institutions as in a universal banking system the need for these types of protection is reduced. If a stock market is the primary mechanism for risk sharing there may be a need for widespread disclosure of information and for rules protecting those with limited self-control and analytical ability.

There have been several successful attempts to promote international regulation. The Basel Committee established by the Group of Ten promotes international cooperation among bank supervisory officials. The Committee has been successful in increasing the exchange of information among members and in developing uniform minimum capital requirements for internationally active banks. The International Organization of Securities Commissions (IOSCO) was established to promote high standards of regulation in order to maintain just, efficient and sound markets by increasing the exchange of information, developing common standards, and ensuring the rigorous enforcement of the standards.

Bankruptcy is a legal process through which organizations restructure their finances. Bankruptcy codes can differ from country to country in areas such as who controls the firm following bankruptcy, whether there is an automatic stay, whether there is renegotiations of old liabilities and provision for new borrowings, and whether old equity holders retain any residual interests. In some countries the primary aim of bankruptcy is to liquidate the firm while in others the goal is to maintain firms as going concerns. In addition to creditors and equity holders, bankruptcy laws must take the needs of employees, customers, and governments into account. Bankruptcy law affects the operations of solvent firms because potential equity investors and creditors take these laws into account when making investment decisions.

The principal regulator of banks in the U.S. is the Federal Reserve System, which was founded in 1913, and operates as the central bank of the United States. The Board of Governors sets reserve requirements for depository institutions, approves discount rates, oversees the Reserve Banks, and administers various regulations concerning such matters as the safety and soundness of banking system, consumer protection and bank mergers. The Federal Reserve directs purchases and sales of securities in the financial markets to expand and contract the money supply. The Reserve Banks are the lenders of last resort for depositary institutions and handle more than one-third of check collections.

Historically there was little regulation of financial markets in the US. Trustees investing others' money were restricted to a list of eligible securities. Dissatisfaction with this legal list approach in the 1930s led to the adoption of the prudent man rule, which states that trustees must "observe how men of prudence, discretion and intelligence manage their own affairs" and act accordingly. In 1911 the U.S. State of Kansas began regulating the issuance of securities within the state. These blue-sky laws were of two types. Merit regulation attempted to judge the investment worth of a security and prohibited the sale of securities deemed too risky. Disclosure regulation concentrated on making the facts available so that investors would have sufficient information to reach an informed decision.

In 1933 the U.S. government began to regulate financial markets. The principal U.S. Federal regulator of financial markets is the Securities and Exchange Commission, an independent, nonpartisan, regulatory agency with responsibility for administering U.S. securities laws. The Securities Act of 1933 requires the provision to investors of all significant information concerning securities that are offered for public sale and prohibits fraud and misrepresentation in the sale of securities.

Questions

1. Consider regulation FD. From the perspective of the regulator, how would this regulation be enforced? Identify three major issues with enforcement?
2. It is said that if you want to make driving safer, place a sharp knife pointing out of every steering wheel. Everyone will then drive no faster than 2 miles per hour. While driving is safer, the economic and social costs are substantial. How should regulators select the proper level of punishment for a violation? What goals should be balanced with the selection of the level of punishment?
3. Who should carry the cost of regulation, the government or the one being regulated? What are the economic and social tradeoffs between these two extremes?
4. Consider the statement "Financial regulations should be fair." As a regulator, how would you define the term 'fair'? From what perspectives could the concept of fairness be considered? Is there only a single perspective of fairness?
5. What is the difference between merit regulation and disclosure regulation?
6. Should financial regulations be developed to minimize the risk of investments?

References

Aitken, Michael, Amy Kwan, and Thomas H. McInish, 2010, Trading prior to price sensitive announcements, Working paper, Capital Markets Corporative Research Centre, Sidney Australia.

Bailey, Warren, Haitao Li, Connie X. Mao, and Rui Zhong, 2003, Regulation Fair Disclosure and earnings information: Market, analyst, and corporate responses, Journal of Finance 58, 2487-2514.

Beatty, Randolph P., Howard Bunsis, and John R.M. Hand, 1998, The indirect economic penalties in SEC investigations of underwriters, Journal of Financial Economics 50, 151-186.

Benston, George J., 1973, Required disclosure and the stock market: an evaluation of the Securities Exchange Act of 1934, American Economic Review 63, 132-155.

Beranek, William, Robert Boehmer, and Brooke Smith, 1996, Much ado about nothing: absolute priority deviations in Chapter 11, Financial Management 25, 102-109.

Cheng, Hongming, 2008, Insider trading in China: the case for the Chinese Securities Regulatory Commission, Journal of Financial Crime 15, 165-178.

Dobson, John, 1997, The role of ethics in finance, Financial Analysts Journal 49, 57-61.

Dobson, John, 1997, Ethics in finance II, Financial Analysts Journal 53, 15-25.

Eleswarapu, Venkat R., Rex Thompson and Kumar Venkataraman, 2004, The impact of Regulation Fair Disclosure: Trading costs and information asymmetry, Journal of Financial and Quantitative Analysis 39, 209-225.

Fodor, Bryan. 2008, Measuring market integrity: a proposed Canadian approach, Journal of Financial Crime 15, 261-268.

Franks, Julian R., Kjell G. Nyborg, and Walter N. Torous, 1996, A comparison of US, UK, and German insolvency codes, Financial Management 25, 86-101.

Gorton, Gary, and Frank A. Schmid, 1996, Universal banking and the performance of German firms, Working paper, University of Pennsylvania, Philadelphia.

Gottschalk, Petter, 2010, Categories of financial crime, Journal of Financial Crime 17, 441-458.

Bill Hu, Thomas McInish, Li Zeng, 2009, The CAN-SPAM Act of 2003 and stock spam emails, Financial Services Review 18, 87–104.

Hu, Bill, Thomas H. McInish, and Lilly Zeng, 2010, Gambling in penny stocks: The case of stock spam emails International Journal of Cyber Criminology 4, 610–629.

International Organization of Securities Commissions, 2003, Objectives and Principles of Securities Regulation, Madrid.

Jensen, Michael C., and William H. Meckling, 1976, Theory of the firm: managerial behavior, agency costs and ownership structure, Journal of Financial Economics 3, 305-360.

Kester, W. Carl, 1994, Banks in the board room: the American versus Japanese and German experiences, Global Finance Journal 5, 181-204.

LeClair, Debbie Thorne, O.C. Ferrell, and John P. Fraedrich, 1998, Integrity Management. Tampa: FL: University of Tampa Press.

Longhofer, Stanley D., 1977, Absolute priority rule violations, credit rationing, and efficiency, Journal of Financial Intermediation 6, 249-267.

Lye, Charmaine and Rosalind Lazar, eds., 1991, The Regulation of Financial and Capital Markets. Singapore: SNP Publishers for the Singapore Academy of Law.

Macey, Jonathan R., and Maureen O'Hara, 1997, The law and economics of best execution, Journal of Financial Intermediation 6, 188-223.

Macey, Jonathan R., and Geoffrey P. Miller, 1991, Origin of the Blue Sky laws, Texas Law Review 70, 347-397.

MacIntyre, Alasdair, 1984, After virtue: a study in moral theory, 2nd ed. Notre Dame, IN: University of Notre Dame Press.

Muhtaseb, Majed R. Chun Chun "Sylvia" Yang, 2008, Portraits of five hedge fund fraud cases, Journal of Financial Crime 15, 179-213.

McInish, Thomas H, Alex Frino, and Frank Sensenbrenner, 2011, Strategic illegal insider trading prior to price sensitive announcements, Journal of Financial Crime 18, 247-253.

Miller, Merton H., 1986, Behavioral rationality in finance: the case of dividends, Journal of Business 59, 451-468.

Organization for Economic Cooperation and Development, 1992, Banks Under Stress. OECD: Paris.

Shefrin, Hersh and Meir Statman, 1993, Ethics, fairness and efficiency in financial markets, Financial Analyst Journal 49, 21-29.

Smith, Clifford W., Jr., Economics and ethics: the case of Salomon Brothers, Financial Management Collection 7, 3-7.

Smith, Craig S., 1999, Bankruptcy in China proves maze to creditors, Wall Street Journal, pp. A8, A9.

Solaiman, S. M., 2009, Investor protection by securities regulators in the primary share markets in Australia and Bangladesh: A comparison and contrast, Journal of Financial Crime 16, 305-333.

Solomon, Robert C., 192, Corporate roles, personal virtues: an Aristotelian approach to business ethics, Business Ethics Quarterly 2, 317-339.

Van Hulle, Cynthia, 1996, On the nature of European holding groups, Working paper, Katholieke Universiteit Leuven, Leuven.

CPSIA information can be obtained at www.ICGtesting.com
Printed in the USA
LVOW05s0607191114

414478LV00004B/20/P

9 781492 887171